my first
CHRISTMAS
CRAFT BOOK

my first CHRISTMAS CRAFT BOOK

35 fun festive projects
for children aged 7+

CICO Kidz

Published in 2016 by CICO Kidz
An imprint of Ryland Peters & Small Ltd
20–21 Jockey's Fields   341 E 116th St
London WC1R 4BW   New York, NY 10029

www.rylandpeters.com

10 9 8 7 6 5 4 3 2 1

Text © CICO Books 2016, plus the project makers listed
on page 128
Design, photography, and illustration ©
CICO Books 2016

A CIP catalog record for this book is available from the
Library of Congress and the British Library.

ISBN: 978 1 78249 381 5

Printed in China

Series consultant: Susan Akass
Editor: Katie Hardwicke
Designer: Barbara Zuñiga
Illustrator: Rachel Boulton
Character illustrations: Hannah George
Template illustrations: Stephen Dew

In-house editor: Dawn Bates
In-house designer: Fahema Khanam
Art director: Sally Powell
Production controller: Mai-ling Collyer
Publishing manager: Penny Craig
Publisher: Cindy Richards

For photography credits, see page 128

Contents

Introduction

Christmas is coming and you can hardly wait! What better time to get busy with a whole range of different craft activities to make your Christmas special. **My First Christmas Craft Book** is the place to start.

My First Christmas Craft Book is divided into four chapters—For the Tree, For your Home, Festive Cards and Wrap, and Treat Time—to cover every aspect of preparing for the holidays. There's no need to buy baubles for your tree or streamers for your room—make your own unique decorations, from a mini tree to popcorn

garlands. Rather than send store-bought cards or wrap presents in store-bought paper, personalize your gifts with your very own designs—try potato printing and stamping. Then get cooking and make delicious treats to delight your family and friends—make truffles to give as gifts and cookies to hang from the tree—and ensure that the build up to Christmas is about so much more than shopping.

To help you get started we have graded all the projects with one, two, or three smiley faces. Level One projects are the easiest and you should be able to manage these without any adult help. These projects use craft materials that you may well already have at home. Level Two projects are a little trickier and sometimes need some adult help, for instance when using the stove. Level Three projects are more challenging and will take longer. You will need to buy special materials online or at a craft store for these projects. Finally, look through the techniques section at the start of the book to guide you through any new skills you may need, so that every project is a success.

So what are you waiting for? Start crafting your way to Christmas!

Project Levels

Level 1

Easy projects that don't
need any adult help.

Level 2

Projects that are a little trickier
and might need some adult help.

Level 3

Longer, more challenging projects
that use special materials which
you will have to order online or
buy from craft stores.

Getting Started

For all the projects, you will need some basic materials:

Equipment

Pencils
Ruler
Set square
Pencil sharpener
Erasers
Fine felt-tipped pens
Acrylic paints
Wide and fine paintbrushes
Palette or plate for mixing paint
Water pot or jar
Glitter
Pair of sharp scissors
Decorative edge craft scissors
Glue stick
White (PVA) glue and spreader
Masking tape
Double-sided tape
Sticky tac
Paper clips

Recycling box

Greetings cards
Gift wrap
Cardboard packaging
Old newspapers and magazines
  (ask first before you cut them up!)

Kitchen cabinet

Cookie cutters
Writing icing
Toothpicks (cocktail sticks)
Rolling pin
Baking sheets
Greaseproof baking parchment

Paper and card

White and colored paper
White and colored card
Colored tissue paper
Tracing paper
Squared math paper
Paper towels

Sewing stash

Sewing needles and thread
Pins
Pinking shears
Embroidery floss (thread)
Yarn (wool)
Scraps of fabric and felt
Ribbons and braid
Buttons and beads

Craft Techniques

These techniques will help you to make your Christmas crafts quickly and easily, with great-looking results.

Copying templates

For some of the projects you need to copy the template onto paper or card before you can cut it out and use it to draw around. You can copy the templates by photocopying them and then cutting out the copy. Some templates may have to be enlarged and the easiest way is on a photocopier—follow the percentage enlargement given with the template.

If you don't have a photocopier, or if you need to transfer the template shape, you can do this using tracing paper as shown here.

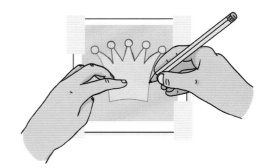

1 Once you have the template to the right size, place a sheet of tracing paper over the template and hold it in place with masking tape. Trace the lines with a hard 4 (2H) pencil.

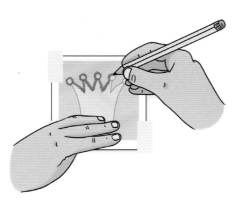

2 Turn the tracing paper over so that the back is facing you and neatly scribble over the lines with a softer pencil, such as a 2 (HB).

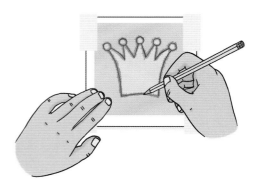

3 Turn the tracing paper over again so that the top is facing you and position it on your paper or card (use masking tape to hold it in place). Carefully draw over the lines you made in step 1 with the hard pencil, and then remove the tracing paper. This will transfer the pencil underneath to give you a nice, clear outline.

Making stencils

Several projects use stencils. You will need a piece of stiff card that has a shiny surface on one side, such as from a cereal package or tissue box, to make the stencil. The shiny side will protect the stencil from getting too wet when you paint over it, so that you can use it again.

1 Copy the template and draw around it on the back of a piece of shiny card. Insert the points of sharp scissors into the middle of the shape and cut out to the edges. Cut away the shape to leave a window.

2 Hold the stencil in place with paper clips, masking tape, or sticky tac. Apply paint or glue with a short, stiff brush, holding the brush at right angles to the card and dabbing. Remove the stencil carefully.

Making your own cards

You can buy greeting card blanks in craft stores or online, but it is also very easy to make your own.

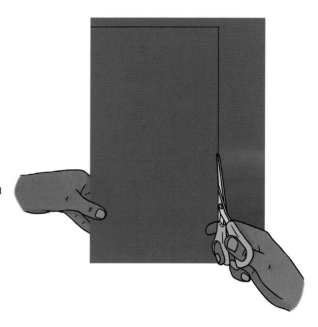

1 Decide on the size of your greeting card and then cut out a rectangle from the card, remembering to double the width. For example, for a folded card that is 5 in. (13 cm) wide and 7 in. (18 cm) tall, you need to measure a rectangle 10 in. (26 cm) wide.

2 Measure along the width to find the center point and mark this on the top and bottom edges.

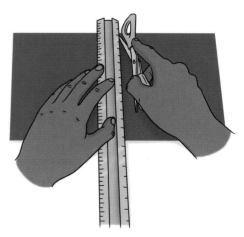

3 You may want to ask an adult to help you with this stage. Place your ruler between the two marks and score along it using the edge of a pair of scissors (score means to mark a line along the cardboard using scissors, but not to cut all the way through). Now fold the card in half along the scored line.

Making a bow

Christmas is a great time for bows—to
decorate presents, to finish a cracker, tied to
the tree—so here are some simple instructions
to help you to tie the perfect bow.

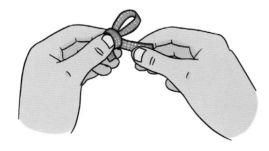

1 Make a loop in the ribbon and wrap the
other end of the ribbon around, as if
tying your shoelace.

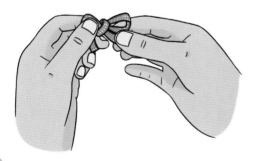

2 Feed the wrapped ribbon
through the hole, and tighten
both loops to make a bow.

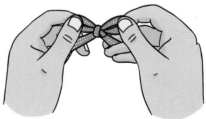

3 Adjust the ends until your bow is neat
and symmetrical.

Sewing Techniques

You don't need to be an expert at sewing to make the projects in this book. All the sewing techniques are easy to learn and do.

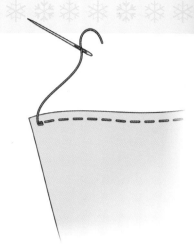

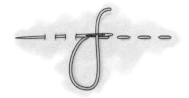

Threading a needle

Thread your needle with about 25 in. (65 cm) of thread or yarn (wool). Pull about 6 in. (15 cm) of the thread through the needle. Tie two knots on top of each other at the other end.

Running stitch

This makes a neat stitch when you are sewing two layers of fabric together. Secure the end of the thread with a few small stitches. Push the needle down through the fabric a little way along, then bring it back up through the fabric at the same distance along. Repeat to form a row of equal stitches.

Finishing stitching

It is important to finish off all your stitching so that it doesn't come undone. When you have finished stitching, sew a few tiny stitches over and over in the same place on the back of the fabric. Then trim off your thread.

Blanket stitch

This makes a pretty edge when you are sewing two layers of fabric together.

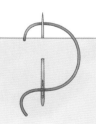

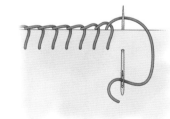

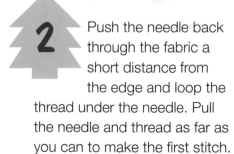

1 Bring the needle through at the edge of the fabric.

2 Push the needle back through the fabric a short distance from the edge and loop the thread under the needle. Pull the needle and thread as far as you can to make the first stitch.

3 Make another stitch to the right of this and again loop the thread under the needle. Continue along the fabric and finish with a few small stitches or a knot on the underside.

Gathering

1. To gather a piece of fabric, knot your thread and begin with a few small stitches over and over in the same place on the fabric to hold the thread firmly so it won't pull through.

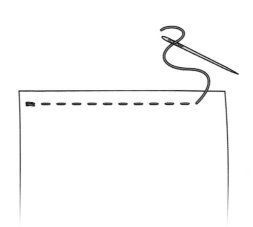

2. Now sew a line of running stitches—the smaller the stitches, the smaller the gathers you will make.

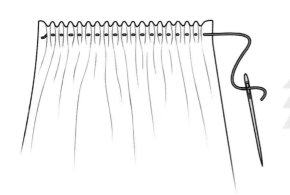

3. At the end, don't finish off; leave the thread loose. Pull the fabric back along the line of stitches so it gathers up into folds.

4. When it is the right size, secure the end of the thread with a few stitches over and over in the same place so the fabric can't come ungathered.

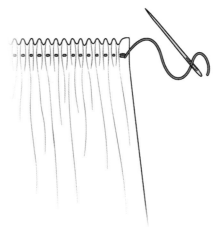

Cooking Techniques

When in the kitchen, these instructions will help you to stay safe
and cook with confidence to make delicious festive treats.

KITCHEN SAFETY

Read this before you start cooking!

• Always wash your hands before you start cooking
and after touching raw meat.

• Tie long hair back so that it is out of the way.

• Wear an apron to keep your clothes clean.

• Make sure your ingredients are fresh and within
their use-by date.

• When using sharp knives, electrical equipment,
or the stovetop (hob), microwave, or oven, always
ask an adult to help you.

• Use oven mitts when holding hot pans or dishes.

• Use a cutting board when using a sharp knife
or metal cookie cutters—this protects the work
surface and will help to stop the knife or cutter
from slipping.

• Keep your work surface clean and wipe up any
spills on the floor so that you don't slip.

• Don't forget to clear up afterward!

Using an oven

Some of the recipes in this book use the oven to
cook the food. For these recipes the first thing
you must do is turn on the oven. This is because
the oven needs to be hot enough to cook the
food you put into it and it takes a little while to
heat up.

• Always ask an adult before using the oven.
• The recipe instructions always tell you at what
temperature to set your oven. Ask an adult to
show you how to set the oven to the correct
temperature.
• On most ovens there is a light, which goes out
when the oven reaches the temperature you
have set, and then it is ready to use.
• Always use oven mitts when putting food into
the oven or taking it out. Even when the dish
you put in is cold, you can easily burn yourself
on the hot racks or the oven door.
• When you take a hot dish out of the oven,
always put it onto a heatproof board or trivet so
that you don't burn the work surface.
• Whenever you cook food in the oven, you need
to be sure that the food doesn't stick to the
oven dish or pan. For cakes and cookies, line
the pan with some baking parchment. To do
this, stand the pan on the parchment and draw
around it to get
the correct size
paper. Cut out
the shape of the
pan and put the
paper in the pan.

Using the stovetop (hob)

You must always have an adult with you when using the stovetop.

- If you are not tall enough to work safely at the stovetop, you must use a small step to stand on, with an adult helping you.
- When using the stovetop, make sure that saucepan handles don't stick out over the front of the stovetop where you could knock into them and knock off the pan.
- Don't have the heat too high—it is easy to burn your food.
- When a pan of water begins to boil, turn down the heat so it doesn't spill all over the stovetop.
- Always remember to turn off the heat when you've finished cooking.
- When you take a pan off the stovetop, always put it onto a heatproof board or trivet so that you don't burn the work surface.

Weighing and measuring

When you are cooking you will often have to weigh or measure ingredients. For baking recipes (such as making a cake), you need to be very accurate or they won't work, but for most cooking, exact measurements are not so important.

This book uses two different types of measurements: one for children in the USA, and one for children in the UK. Follow one type of measurement all the way through a recipe and don't swap between the two—use either all the first measurements given (USA style) or all the second ones, which are in brackets (UK style.) You will need measuring cups or weighing scales for large quantities, measuring spoons for small quantities, and measuring cups or a pitcher (jug) for liquids.

Rolling out pastry dough

- Use plenty of flour on your work surface to stop the pastry sticking to the surface. Put some on your rolling pin too.
- When you roll pastry, push down and away from you.
- Keep moving the pastry, to make sure it hasn't stuck, and add a little more flour if it does stick.
- Try not to handle the pastry too much—it needs to stay cold and your hands will make it hot!

chapter 1
For Your Tree

Pompom Baubles

Pompoms are fun and easy to make, and you can use them to create these cute, fluffy Christmas tree baubles. They look like snowballs when made in white yarn, but you could make them in lots of colors to add some bright decorations to your tree.

You will need

Template on page 120

Paper

Pencil

Scissors

Thick card

White knitting yarn (wool)

Red 3-D fabric pen

Approximately 4 in. (10 cm) gingham ribbon per bauble

1 Trace the pompom disc template on page 120 and cut it out carefully. Cut out the hole in the middle. Draw two of the discs on thick card and cut them out.

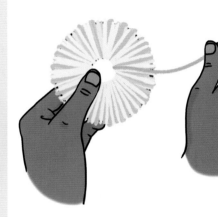

2 Cut a length of yarn about 2¼ yd. (2 m) long and wind it into a loose ball that will fit through the middle holes of the discs. Put the two cardboard discs together and begin to wind the yarn around the cardboard, pushing it through the center hole and back over the outside.

3 When you reach the end of the yarn, cut another length, tie it to the first length, and continue to wind the yarn. Keep winding, building up layers of yarn all the way round the discs until there is no more room in the middle to push the yarn through. The more layers there are, the fluffier the pompom.

4 Now, holding the pompom discs firmly together, push the points of your scissors down through the yarn and between the card discs. Cut the yarn all around the edge of the discs—this is quite hard work! Keep holding the discs together as you cut.

5 Cut a length of yarn about 8 in. (20 cm) long. Hold one end in one hand and thread the other end between the two cardboard discs. Wind it round tightly twice and then tie the two ends together in a tight knot. Leave the loose ends to make the hanging loop for the pompom.

6 Gently pull the cardboard discs away from the pompom. If this is difficult, you could cut them off but then you will have to make more discs if you want more pompoms! Trim any bits of yarn that are too long, and fluff the pompom to give it a nice round shape.

7 Use a 3-D fabric pen to draw tiny dots on the pompom. Tie the long ends together with a knot to make a loop and finish by tying the ribbon in a bow around the hanging loop. See page 13 for how to tie a bow.

Peg-doll Fairy

This fairy is very special and so you will need to buy some very special materials to make her—but it will be worth it when you see her shining and magical at the top of the Christmas tree.

You will need

Round wooden clothespin (peg)

Acrylic paints for skin and hair

Fine paintbrush

Fine marker pen

Gold organza

Scissors, needle, and thread

White (PVA) glue

24 in. (60 cm) of 1½-in. (35-mm) wide gold organza ribbon

Flower sequin for her hair

Star sequin and string of tiny sequins for the wand

Gold sequins

Ribbon, about 16 in. (40 cm) long

1 Paint the top of the clothespin with flesh-colored paint. When it is dry, paint on the hair and draw on the eyes and mouth with a fine pen.

2 Cut two pieces of organza, each measuring 9 x 4 in. (22 x 10 cm). Thread your needle. Lay one piece of organza on top of the other and, close to the top edge, sew a few stitches to stop the thread from pulling through. Then sew running stitches (see page 14) along the top through both layers. Pull the thread to gather up the material (see page 15), making sure that it fits around the clothespin. Finish with a few stitches to hold the gathers in place.

3 Wrap the skirt around the clothespin and stitch it together at the back. A dab of glue will help to hold it in place. Leave the glue to dry.

4 Fold the gold ribbon in half lengthwise. Dab glue around the body of the clothespin and wrap the ribbon around it, tying it at the back. Let it dry. Open out the rest of the ribbon and cut the ends into a V-shape.

5 Tie the ribbon into a big bow (see page 13) to look like wings.

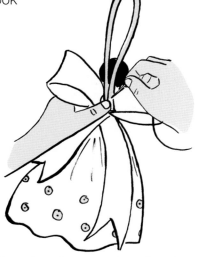

6 Finish off by using the sequins. Glue a flower sequin to the hair. Make a wand from the string of tiny sequins and a star sequin, and glue it in place. Glue gold sequins onto the skirt. Stitch a ribbon to the back of the fairy, so that you can tie her to the tree.

Button Tree

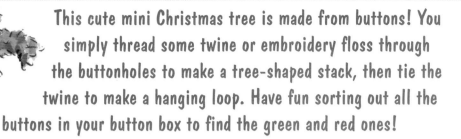

This cute mini Christmas tree is made from buttons! You simply thread some twine or embroidery floss through the buttonholes to make a tree-shaped stack, then tie the twine to make a hanging loop. Have fun sorting out all the buttons in your button box to find the green and red ones!

You will need

10–15 green buttons, ranging from ½–1¼ in. (1–3 cm) in diameter

4 small red buttons, about ½ in. (1 cm) in diameter

1 yellow star bead

8 in. (20 cm) embroidery floss (thread) or baker's twine

White (PVA) glue

1 Select your green buttons and line them up from largest to smallest. Have your red buttons and yellow star bead ready, too.

2 Take an 8-in. (20-cm) piece of embroidery floss (thread) or baker's twine and, using your fingertips, rub a tiny amount of glue on the first ½ in. (1 cm) of each end of the thread. Let it dry. This will stiffen the twine so that it doesn't unravel as you thread the buttons.

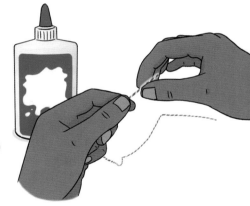

3 To make the tree you start from the bottom and work to the top. Push the twine up through both holes of the first red button. Make sure the button sits halfway along so that the two ends of the twine are the same length.

 4 Next, add the three remaining red buttons one by one, threading one end of twine through each hole. Keep the twine ends equal.

5 Now add the green buttons, starting with the largest and ending with the smallest. If some of your buttons have four holes, use two holes that are diagonally opposite each other. Make sure that all the buttons are pulled down firmly on top of one another and then thread on the yellow star at the top with both ends through one hole in the bead. Pull it down on top of the buttons and check that the twine ends are still equal lengths.

 6 Knot the ends of the twine together at the top to make a loop and your button tree is ready to hang.

Stack up those BUTTONS

Hanging Felt Stars

Cut out from red and green felt using pinking shears, these jolly tree decorations are an ideal easy sewing project. We decorated the star shapes with pretty buttons and hung them from ricrac braid loops.

You will need

Template on page 121

Paper and pencil

Scissors

Colored felt or Christmas fabric

Pins

Pinking shears

6 in. (15 cm) red ricrac braid per star

Needle and matching cotton thread

Fiberfill stuffing

White (PVA) glue

Assorted pearl buttons (about 8 per star)

1 Copy the star template on page 121 onto paper and cut it out. Fold the felt in half, as you will need two star shapes per decoration. Pin the paper star motif to the felt to hold it in place. Use a pencil to draw around the star motif.

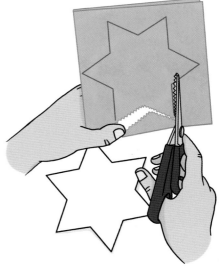

2 Remove the motif, but pin the two pieces of felt together again before you start cutting. Using pinking shears, carefully cut all the way around the star shape, making sure you are cutting through both layers of fabric. The pinking shears give a pretty zigzag effect to the edges. Cut out as many stars as you want to make.

3 To make the hanging loop, fold a 6-in. (15-cm) length of ricrac braid in half and place it between the two layers of felt at the top of one of the points. Thread the needle. Start with a few small stitches in the top layer of felt to secure the thread and then push the needle through the two layers of felt and the end of the braid. Sew two or three stitches through all four layers in the same place to secure the loop.

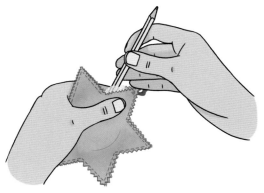

4 Continue stitching around the points of the star, using small running stitches (see page 14) about ¼ in. (5 mm) from the edge. Leave one side of the last point open for the stuffing.

5 Take small pieces of stuffing and carefully push them into the opening. You may need to use the end of a pencil to make sure that the stuffing is pushed right into all the points of the star. Add enough stuffing to fill the shape well.

6 Hold the two layers of felt together and stitch the opening closed, using the same small running stitches. Finish off by making two or three stitches together, and trim the thread.

Tip

Use sequins or beads to decorate the shape for a sparkly festive look.

7 Use dabs of glue to stick the buttons to the front of the star and let them dry completely. You can add some buttons to the back, too, if you like, but only when the first side is completely dry.

Orange Slice Decorations

These unusual tree decorations are made from dried slices of fresh orange. They still smell of oranges and this will combine with the scent of your pine tree to fill your house with the fragrance of Christmas.

You will need

Fresh oranges

Sharp knife

Cutting board

Paper towels

Baking sheet

Oven mitts

Wooden skewer

6 in. (15 cm) gingham ribbon (½ in./1 cm wide) for each hanging loop

Scissors

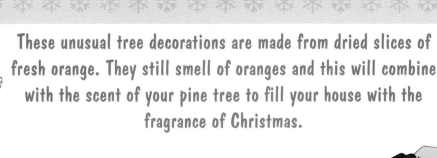

1 Put an orange on the cutting board and hold it firmly with your fingers in a claw position so they are well away from the knife. Make sure that the end of the orange is pointing sideways not up—you want the star shape of the segments when you cut it. Carefully cut slices about ¼ in. (5 mm) wide. You may like to ask an adult to help you with cutting the slices, especially as the piece of orange you are holding gets smaller.

2 Lay the slices on pieces of paper towel and blot them with another sheet of paper towel to remove any juice. This will speed up the drying process.

3 Ask an adult to help you to turn the oven on to the very lowest setting. Lay the orange slices on the baking sheet and put them in the oven for about 4 hours, or until they are completely dry. Use oven mitts to remove the baking sheet from the oven—take care as it will be hot.

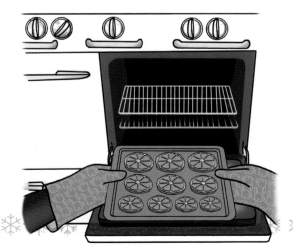

4 Once the baking sheet has completely cooled, remove the orange slices from the sheet and set them aside for finishing. The slices should be hard and dry, but still smell citrussy (like oranges).

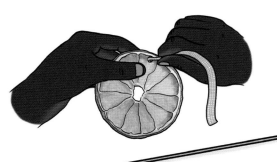

5 Carefully make a small hole near the edge of each orange slice using a sharp point, such as a wooden skewer. Thread the ribbon through the hole and tie the ends in a knot. Trim the ribbon ends diagonally with scissors to prevent them from fraying.

Tip
Make sure that the slices "cook" long enough to dry completely, otherwise they won't keep for long and may go moldy.

Surprising CITRUS slices

Pompom Angels

These sweet little angels, with their delicate paper-doily wings and golden haloes, are a twist on the traditional woolen pompom. We have made them in soft pastel colors but you can use any color yarn to make a pretty Christmas decoration for the tree.

You will need

Templates on page 120

Scissors

Pale pink, blue, or white yarn (wool)

White (PVA) glue

Small paper doily

3 small pearl beads for the angel's eyes and mouth

Gold pipe cleaner for the halo

1 Trace the pompom disc templates on page 120 and cut them out carefully. Cut out the hole in the middle. Draw two large and two small discs on thick card and cut them out.

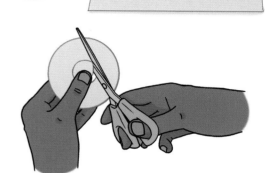

2 Cut a length of yarn about 2.2 yd. (2 m) long and wind it into a loose ball that will fit through the middle holes of the discs. Now turn to pages 20–21 and follow steps 2–5 of the Pompom Baubles to make your first pompom but don't trim the ends of the yarn you tie it together with—leave them long.

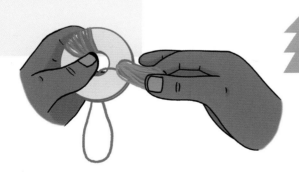

3 Now make another smaller pompom using the two smaller discs for the angel's head. Use the loose yarn ends of the two pompoms to tie them together, pull tightly, and knot the yarn several times before trimming the ends with scissors.

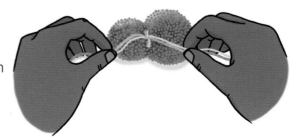

4 Fold the paper doily in half, crease it, and cut along the crease with scissors to make two semicircles. Fold each semicircle in half again to make a triangular wing, and then glue the points of the wings to the center back of the larger pompom.

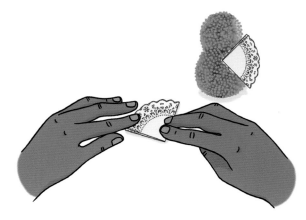

5 Use dots of glue to stick the pearl eyes and mouth to the front of the smaller pompom, which forms the angel's head.

The prettiest POMPOMS

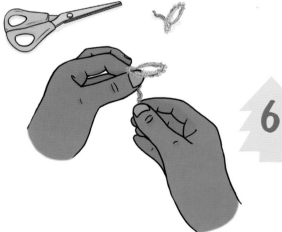

6 To make the halo, form a circular shape, about 1 in. (2.5 cm) in diameter, with the gold pipe cleaner. Twist the ends to secure them in place and trim them with scissors.

7 Stick the halo to the top of the angel's head with glue. To hang your angel, attach a length of yarn around the neck and tie to make a hanging loop.

Mini Tree

Here's your chance to decorate your very own tree in miniature! Decorate the pot, make some candy canes, add some cute mini pompoms and baubles, and finish it with ribbons and bows. You can keep it in your room or use it as a decorative centerpiece for your dining table.

You will need

Miniature living Christmas tree in a pot or artificial tree with a stand

Terra-cotta pot (big enough for your tree and its pot or stand to fit into)

Paintbrushes

Undercoat paint

Silver paint

1 yd. (1 m) gingham ribbon (1 in./2.5 cm wide)

Sharp pointed scissors

White (PVA) glue

Red and white pipe cleaners

1 yd. (1 m) silver ribbon (¼ in./5 mm wide)

Red and silver miniature pompoms (see page 20 to make your own)

2.2 yd. (2 m) gingham ribbon (½ in./1 cm) wide

Miniature baubles

1 Paint a layer of undercoat on the terra-cotta pot and let it dry completely. Now paint a coat of silver paint and let it dry. If it looks streaky, paint on a second coat of silver paint and let it dry.

2 Stand your tree inside the silver pot. Measure a length of the wider gingham ribbon to fit around the top of the pot. Add about 1 in. (2.5 cm) for overlap, and cut it. Glue it around the rim of the pot.

3 Tie a neat bow from the same ribbon (see page 13) and glue it to the pot on the ribbon border, to hide the ends. Let the glue dry.

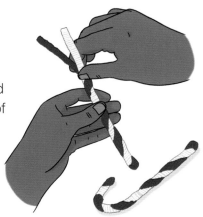

4 To make candy canes, twist the bottom ends of a red and white pipe cleaner together so they are attached. Now wind them together for a striped effect. Carefully bend one end of the twisted pipe cleaners to form a candy-cane shape with a curved top. Now they can simply be hooked onto the Christmas tree.

5 To make a hanging loop for the pompoms, cut a 2½-in. (6-cm) length of narrow silver ribbon. Fold it in half and hold the ends together to form a loop. Apply a small dab of glue between the ends to hold them in place. Let the glue dry.

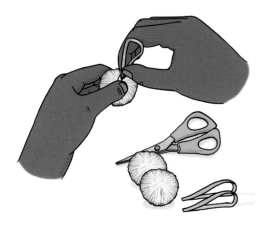

6 Using a pair of pointed scissors, carefully snip open a pompom so that you can see the center. Apply a dab of glue to the middle of the pompom and push in the end of the loop you made in step 5. Press the two sides of the opening closed. Allow the glue to dry completely before hanging the pompoms from the tree. Add some mini baubles, too.

TRANSFORM a tiny tree

Tip

When making bows, cut the ends of ribbon on the diagonal to prevent them from fraying.

7 To finish your tree, cut lengths of the narrower gingham ribbon and tie them into bows (see page 13) on the ends of the branches of the Christmas tree. Cut an 8-in. (20-cm) length of the wider gingham ribbon and tie it around the top of the Christmas tree to make a tree topper.

Cookie Cutter Clay Decorations

Using cookie cutters to cut shapes out of clay gives a lovely crisp outline. These clay decorations have all the charm of gingerbread cookies but, once you've made them, they'll last forever!

You will need

Package of quick-drying clay

Rolling pin

Christmas cookie cutters—we used an angel, tree, and reindeer

Pencil

Acrylic paints

Paintbrushes

Narrow colored and patterned ribbons

1 Roll out the clay on a flat surface as if you were rolling out cookie dough, until it is about ⅛ in. (3 mm) thick. Using the cookie cutters, cut out your shapes.

2 Make a hole at the top of each shape with a pencil or the end of a small paintbrush. Make sure that your holes are big enough to push the ribbon through. Let the shapes dry. This could take 24 hours, so allow plenty of time. The warmer the room, the quicker the drying time.

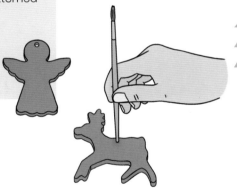

3 Paint the top of the shapes, let the paint dry, and then turn over and paint the other side. Acrylic paint is quick-drying, so you won't need to wait long.

Cut...PAINT...hang

4 Fold the ribbon in half and push the folded part through the hole in your shape, from back to front. Thread the ends through the loop at the front and then gently pull tight. Tie the ribbon ends and the decorations are ready to hang.

Tip
Using long lengths of pretty ribbon to hang the shapes makes them look even more decorative.

chapter 2
For Your Home

Snow Globes

Festive snow globes make great gifts for friends and family, and they are lots of fun to make.

You will need

Empty, clean glass jars with lids

Sandpaper (optional)

Silver paint

Paintbrush

Strong waterproof glue or waterproof tile adhesive

Christmas decorations to put in jar

Pitcher (jug) and spoon for pouring

Distilled water

Glycerin

Clear dishwashing detergent

Glitter

Silicon sealant (optional)

1 Paint the lid of the jar (you may wish to sand it lightly before painting) with silver paint and let it dry completely. If required, apply a second coat of paint for better coverage and again let it dry.

2 Use strong glue to attach the decoration to the inside of the jar lid. If the decoration is on the small side, build up a small mound using waterproof tile adhesive and press the decoration firmly into this. Leave until completely dry.

3 Use a pitcher (jug) to pour the distilled water into the jam jar. Fill it almost to the brim. Stir in two teaspoons of glycerin and half a teaspoon of dishwashing detergent. Add five or six spoonfuls of glitter to the water. White or silver glitter looks most similar to snow, although bright colors like red or green can look very jolly and festive.

Let it SNOW!

4 Carefully place the lid on the top of the jar and screw the lid tightly in place. Turn the jar upside down, so the Christmas decoration is the right way up.

Tip

• For a better finish, sand the lid lightly before painting.

• The jar should be watertight, but you may wish to seal it around the edges with a thin layer of silicon sealant.

Advent Gift Buckets

Make these tiny buckets into a very special advent calendar that you could use every year as you countdown to Christmas Day. The buckets are decorated with little stenciled hearts, ribbons, and a special numbered clothespin (peg). With twenty-four buckets to decorate, there's lots to keep you busy crafting for a couple of days.

You will need

Template on page 121

Paper and pencil

Card for stencil—use shiny-coated card from a packaging box

Sharp pointed scissors

24 small metal buckets, approximately 2 in. (5 cm) high

Masking tape

Green and red paint

Stencil brush or thick paintbrush

Narrow ribbon or ricrac braid, approximately ½ in. (1 cm) wide

White (PVA) glue

Christmas tissue paper

Foil-wrapped chocolates and candy canes or tiny gifts

Numbered Advent calendar clothespins (pegs) or 24 plain clothespins (pegs)

1 Copy the template on page 121 and use it to make a stencil from the shiny card, following the instructions on page 11. Make a second stencil exactly the same.

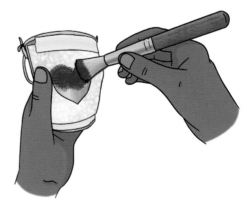

2 With the shiny side facing out, lay one stencil over the front of a bucket and use small pieces of masking tape to hold it in place. Paint inside the heart using red paint. Dab it on with the brush at right angles to the bucket so that the paint doesn't spread behind the card. Keep your brush quite dry so that the paint doesn't run.

3 Carefully peel off the stencil and repeat the process on 11 of the other buckets. Check that there is no paint on the back of the stencil before you stick it to the next bucket and wipe it if you need to. When you have stenciled 12 red hearts, wash and dry the brush thoroughly. Use the second stencil to paint green hearts on the other 12 buckets.

4 When the paint is dry, cut a length of ribbon or braid to fit around the bottom of a bucket, adding about ¼ in. (5 mm) for overlap. After you have measured the first one, cut 23 more pieces the same length. Apply a line of glue to the back of the first ribbon and fix it in place, starting at the back of the bucket to hide the ribbon's raw edges. Repeat on the remaining buckets.

5 Cut a small square of tissue paper, measuring approximately 5 x 5 in. (13 x 13 cm). Place the tissue paper in the bucket, to make a liner. Fill with chocolates and candy canes or a small gift.

6 If you have special numbered clothespins (pegs), clip one to the front of each bucket to finish. Otherwise, decorate your own clothespins using pens or stickers and writing on the numbers 1 to 24.

Tip

When you have finished the buckets, either fill them up yourself with candy or gifts, or ask (very nicely) if someone else in your family would fill them for you—that way every day will be a surprise!

Decoupage Letters

Say it with words! Plain papier-mâché letters are perfect for making a cheery decoration, covered in bright Christmas paper and ricrac braid. We spelled NOEL but SNOW, SANTA, or HO HO HO would all look great. The letters are often sold alongside decoupage kits in craft stores or online, and will make a decoration that will keep for years to come.

You will need

An old plate

Large (8 in./20 cm) papier-mâché letters to spell your choice of word

White or undercoat paint

Paintbrush

Scissors

Decoupage tissue paper in Christmas colors or patterns, or gift wrap

Decoupage glue or white (PVA) glue (see tip)

Tablespoon

Ricrac braid (enough to wrap around the sides of each letter)

Small red buttons (optional)

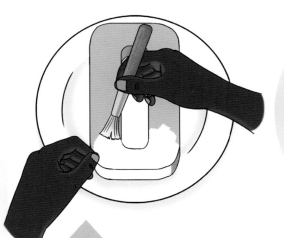

Crafty Tip

You can make your own decoupage glue by mixing 6 tablespoons of white (PVA) glue with 2 tablespoons of water and stirring. together well.

1 Working on an old plate, paint the letters with the white paint or undercoat, and let them dry. This will prevent the brown papier-mâché background from showing through. Wash out the paint from your paintbrush.

2 Use the scissors to cut the patterned tissue paper into small squares and rectangles, measuring about ¾–1¼ in. (2–3 cm). They don't need to be precise. You can also use gift wrap.

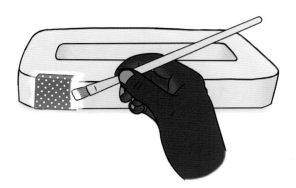

3 Paint a thin layer of glue onto a small patch of the first letter and stick on a square of paper. Press it firmly into place. Paint on some more glue, painting it over the edge of the first square. Stick on the next square so it overlaps the first one.

4 Continue to stick on paper all over the letter, overlapping the pieces so that none of the white paint shows through. Try not to have a piece finishing at an edge of the letter—always fold it over for a neater finish. You may have to crease the paper a little around curved edges. Cover all the letters in the same way.

5 To give your letters a little shine, and to make sure that any flaps of paper are stuck down firmly, paint more glue all over the top of the paper you have glued on. Let the letters dry.

Spell out CHRISTMAS

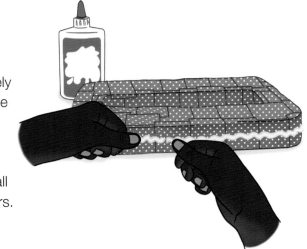

6 Cut a length of white ricrac braid to fit all around the outside of your first letter, plus a little extra as it is difficult to measure accurately around corners. Spread glue (straight from the bottle, not diluted) onto the ricrac and stick it around the letter, pushing it right into any corners. Trim any excess ricrac before you stick down the ends. You could also use small red buttons to decorate the sides of the letters. Do the same to finish the other letters.

Felt Cone Decorations

Using a simple felt cone as your starting point, make a cute miniature Christmas tree decorated with tiny red and green beads to look like baubles, or create a sweet little reindeer. After that, use your imagination based on the same cone design—how about Santa Claus in red and white felt?

You will need

Templates on page 122

Paper and pencil

Scissors

White (PVA) glue

Stapler

For the miniature tree:

Piece of green card

Sheet of green felt

Red and green beads

Green felt ball for the top of the tree

Tiny seed beads for the tree top

For the reindeer:

Piece of brown card

Sheet of brown felt

Piece of white card

Sheet of cream felt

Red pompom for the nose

2 small black buttons for the eyes

To make one miniature tree

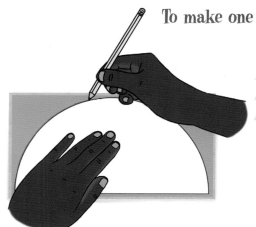

1 Glue the piece of green card onto the felt and allow to dry. Follow steps 1 and 2 on page 50 to cut out a semicircle from the green felt.

2 Roll the semicircle of green felt into a neat cone shape and then fix it into position using the stapler. (You may need to ask an adult to help with this.) You will need to use several staples to keep the shape firmly fixed in place.

3 Start to add the beads to the cone, using a small dab of glue. Use a mix of red and green beads, spacing them evenly around the cone.

CONICAL creations

4 To finish your tree, glue a felt ball to the top of the cone and decorate with tiny seed beads to add some sparkle, if you like.

Tip

Make a row of miniature trees using different shades of green felt—they would look fantastic along a mantelpiece or on the center of the dining table.

To make one reindeer

 Using the templates on page 122, enlarge or trace the cone and antler shapes onto the paper. Cut out all the shapes. Glue the piece of brown card onto the brown felt, and the white card onto the cream felt, and allow to dry.

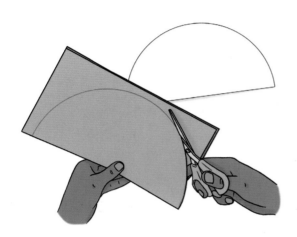

 Position the semicircular cone template on the card side of the brown felt, lining up the straight edges, draw around it with a pencil, and cut out with scissors.

Roll the semicircle of brown felt into a neat cone shape and then fix it into position using the stapler across the join (you may need to ask an adult to help with this). You will need to use several staples to keep the shape firmly fixed in place.

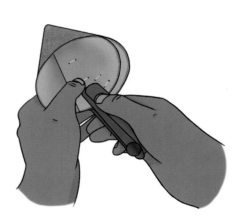

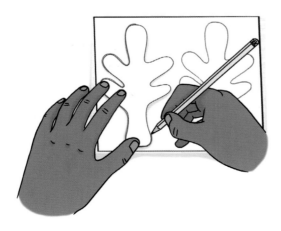

 Position the antler template on the card side of the cream felt, draw around it twice with a pencil, and cut out two antlers. To help cut the fiddly curves, turn the card not the scissors.

5 Spreading glue on the felt side of the antlers, glue them to the back of the cone near the pointed end. While they dry, lie the cone down with the antlers underneath and use something inside to weigh it down—this will help them stick firmly in place.

6 Carefully glue the bright red pompom to the front of the cone to make the reindeer's nose. To finish, glue the two button eyes to the cone.

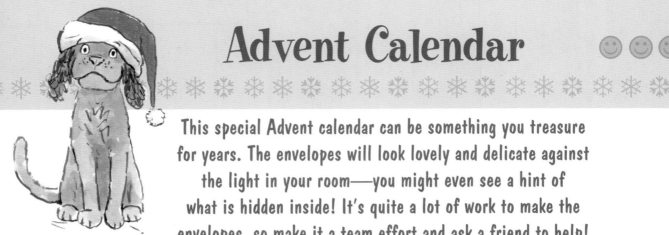

Advent Calendar

This special Advent calendar can be something you treasure for years. The envelopes will look lovely and delicate against the light in your room—you might even see a hint of what is hidden inside! It's quite a lot of work to make the envelopes, so make it a team effort and ask a friend to help!

You will need

Templates on page 123

Paper and pencil

Scissors

Sheets of colored paper (we used blue, green, pink, and gold)

2 large sheets (A2 size, or approx 16½ x 24 in./42 x 60 cm) of heavy-gauge tracing paper or other translucent paper

Ruler (metal is best)

Glue stick

Gold marker pen

25 small gifts or candies

6½ yd. (6 m) gold twine

25 curtain clips, preferably with small hooks

1 Using the templates on page 123, trace the heart, crown, star, tree, and bell shapes onto paper or photocopy them onto thin card. Cut out the shapes and use them as templates to draw around on the colored paper. You need 17 shapes altogether.

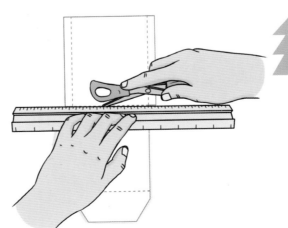

2 Trace the envelope template from page 123 and use this to cut 25 envelopes from translucent paper. Using the edge of a scissor blade against the metal ruler, gently score (see page 12) along the folds of each envelope shape following the dotted lines on the template.

3 Fold along the score lines and run your fingers along the folds to make a sharp crease. Glue along the tabs, fold over the long end, and press the sides firmly together to make an envelope.

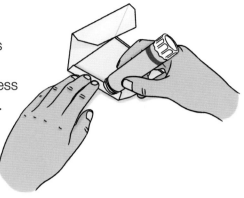

4 With the gold pen, write or trace "Noel" on one envelope and the numbers 1, 4, 8, 12, 16, 20, and 24 on seven of the others. Glue the paper cut-out shapes to the remainder of the envelopes. Place a motto or gift into each package, or ask someone to do it for you so that each day will bring a surprise!

5 Cut the gold twine in half. Leave a length of about 24 in. (60 cm), then tie a small bow in the twine, just like you would if you were tying your laces (see page 13). Now, tie 13 small bows at 4 in. (10 cm) intervals. Repeat with the other piece of twine, tying 12 bows.

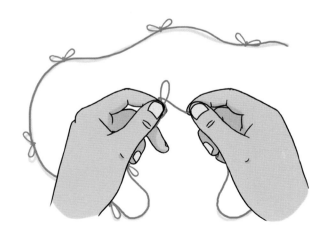

6 Hook a curtain clip into the knot of each bow. Next, clip on the envelopes, starting with the number 1, then two with shapes and no numbers, then number 4, three shapes, number 8, three shapes, and so on, finishing with the Noel envelope for Christmas Day. (You might want to add little numbers onto the shape envelopes to help you know which date you are on.)

7 Tie the two pieces of twine together at both ends so that one hangs beneath the other when you hang it up. Find somewhere special to hang it and then trim the ends of the twine if necessary.

Countdown to CHRISTMAS

Paper Snowflakes

You may have made snowflakes by cutting paper, but with this template you can create a really sophisticated design. After you have used it a few times, change it a little to create your own design. Each one will be unique, just like a real snowflake (though real ones have six points!). These snowflakes add a magical wintery touch hanging at a window, or glue them together to make a tree garland.

You will need

Sheets of white letter size (A4) paper

Scissors

Template on page 124

Tracing paper

Pencil

Paper clip or sticky tac

Glue stick

Needle and thread (optional)

1 Fold up the left bottom corner of the paper so the left side lines up with the top edge. Cut off the spare rectangle of paper. You can use this to make small squares for tiny snowflakes.

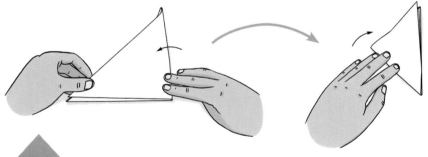

2 Fold the triangle in half. Then fold it in half again.

3 Trace the snowflake design on page 124 onto a piece of tracing paper. Position the tracing with the pencil lines facing the folded paper triangle. Use a paper clip or sticky tac to hold it in place. Draw or scribble firmly over the pencil lines to transfer the snowflake design onto the paper (see also page 10).

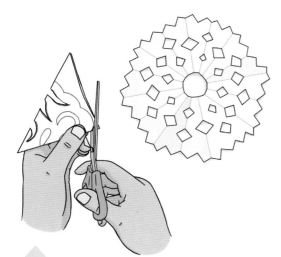

4 Cut out the marked shapes along the pencil lines, including the patterned edge, and then open out the folded paper to reveal your snowflake.

5 Make more snowflakes, changing the template design just a little each time at first and then going on to create your very own designs.

6 Glue the snowflakes together in a row, to create a garland, or use the needle to attach long threads to them to hang at different heights for a wintery window display.

paper snowflakes

Red and White Paper Chains

Everyone loves paper chains! These ones have fun fancy edges and punched designs and by alternating two colors—in this case red and white—you can make them really stylish. This is a great activity to do with a friend so that you can make a really long chain. Take turns doing different tasks.

You will need

12 in. (30 cm) ruler (a narrow one is best)

Pencil

Letter size (A4) sheets of red and white paper

Decorative edge craft scissors

Christmas-design hole punch (make sure the size of the design will fit inside the paper chain)

Glue stick

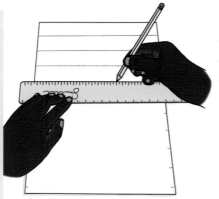

1 If your ruler is narrow enough for a paper chain, just line up the edge with the short edge of the paper and draw along it, then keep going, lining up the ruler edge on the line you have just drawn. If your ruler is too wide to do this, you will need to measure and make a mark every 1¼ in. (3 cm) along both long edges, then join up the marks with your ruler and draw lines across the paper.

2 Now cut out the strips along your marked lines, using decorative edge craft scissors. It's best to measure and cut several strips before you start punching and sticking.

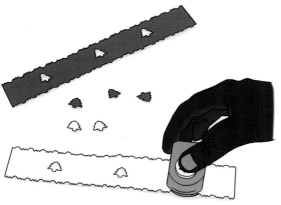

3 Use the Christmas-design hole punch to cut out the designs along each paper chain, spacing them at regular intervals along the chain—we punched 3 holes per chain. Make sure not to punch too close to the ends of the chain.

How **LONG** is your **CHAIN?**

4 Bend the first paper chain to form a loop and glue the ends together, overlapping them by about ½ in. (1 cm). Thread the second paper chain through the first loop and glue the ends together as before.

5 Continue to thread the paper pieces through the last loop to create the chain, making sure you alternate the colors for each loop. How long can you make your chain?

Tip
You can use the cut-out shapes from the hole punch to make table confetti!

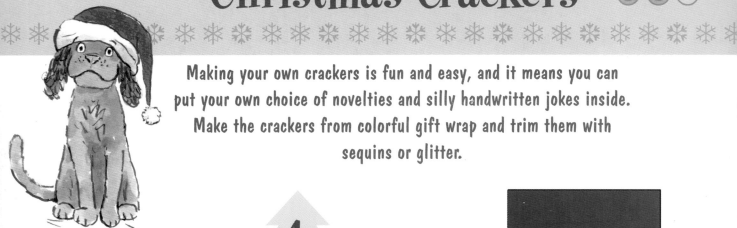

Making your own crackers is fun and easy, and it means you can put your own choice of novelties and silly handwritten jokes inside. Make the crackers from colorful gift wrap and trim them with sequins or glitter.

You will need

Small cardboard rolls

8 x 12 in. (20 x 30 cm) piece of paper per cracker

Pencil, ruler, and scissors

White (PVA) glue or double-sided tape

Snaps for crackers

Gifts, paper hats, and jokes

8 in. (20 cm) ribbon (¼ in./5 mm wide) per cracker

Sequin trim

1 Lay the cardboard roll in the center of the paper and mark the position of each end using a pencil. Set the roll aside.

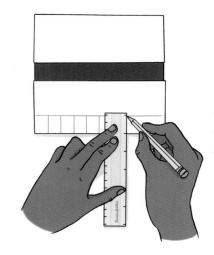

2 Using the marks made on the paper as a guide, fold the paper along the crease, right sides together, and press the folds flat. Using a ruler, mark out lines along the fold about ¾ in. (2 cm) apart and stopping about 1 in. (2.5 cm) in from the outside edge of the paper.

CRACKERS SAFETY

• Crackers snaps are a low-risk fire hazard and must always be used with adult supervision. Never pull a snap on its own.

One ... two ... three... PULL!

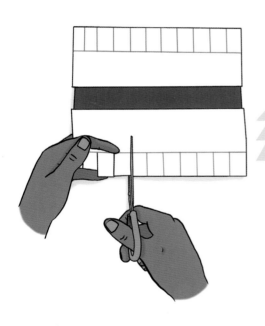

3 Use scissors to cut along the marked lines to create slits in the paper. Repeat on the other side. These slits help the cracker ends to be tied more easily.

4 Now unfold the paper and lay it flat, wrong side facing up. Place the cardboard roll on top. Apply a dab of glue or use a small piece of double-sided tape to hold the paper on the roll. Wrap the paper around the roll as tightly as you can. Apply glue along the whole edge of the paper and press firmly in place. Allow to dry completely.

5 Push the cracker snap through the open end of the roll. This is also the time to insert any small gifts or trinkets, a paper hat, and a joke or other motto.

6 Cut the ribbon in half and tie a length of ribbon around one end of the cracker. Tie in a knot. Repeat at the other end. Trim the ends of the ribbon on the diagonal with scissors, to prevent them fraying.

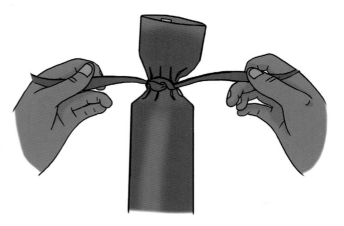

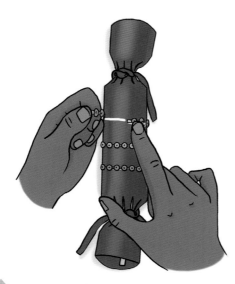

Tip
Crackers are also a fun way of wrapping small gifts—pop the gift in with the cracker snap, then tie a pretty matching gift label to one end of the cracker to finish.

7 Measure the circumference of the cracker and cut three lengths of sequin trim to fit. Glue the sequin trim in rows around the cracker. Allow the glue to dry completely.

Tea Light Table Twinklers

Candles really make things look really Christmassy and these painted jars are great for adding a little sparkle as part of a table setting. Paint old glass jars and pop a tea light candle inside. You can use real candles or, for a safer option, use LED tea lights—then you can keep them twinkling in your bedroom as you wait for Santa to call!

You will need

Clean and dry glass jars

Glass paints in yellow, red, and green

Paintbrush

Paper and pen

Gold glass outliner pen or paint

Tea light candles or LED tea lights

1 Paint your jars. Build up the color by painting one coat, letting it dry, and then painting another coat.

2 Sketch out a few designs on paper until you are happy with your drawing. Keep the design simple, with just a few lines to make the shapes. We drew a simple triangle for a tree, baubles, and snowflakes.

SAFETY FIRST

• Never leave a burning candle or tea light unattended.

Twinkle TWINKLE little tea light

3 Use your gold outliner paint to draw the designs on your jars, repeating the design around the jar so that it looks pretty on all sides. Allow to dry, according to the manufacturer's instructions.

4 Put a tea light candle in each jar and ask an adult to help you to light the candles (or switch on your LED).

Christmas Stocking

Hang up this pretty stocking and you are sure to tempt Santa to fill it with something special. Learning to sew blanket stitch will give you a new skill as you make a Christmas gift to yourself that you can be proud of.

You will need

Templates on page 125

Paper and pencil

Scissors

16 in. (40 cm) cream fleece fabric (44 in./137 cm wide)

Pins

Red patterned felt for heart motif (6 x 6 in./15 x 15 cm)

Needle and red sewing thread

Red embroidery floss (thread)

8 in. (20 cm) gingham fabric (44 in./137 cm wide)

Iron

4 in. (10 cm) gingham ribbon

White (PVA) glue

Pearl button

1 Enlarge the stocking template on page 125 on a photocopier at 200% to make it the right size. Cut out the template. Fold the cream fleece fabric in half and pin the template to the fabric. Cut out the stocking pieces (you will end up with two pieces).

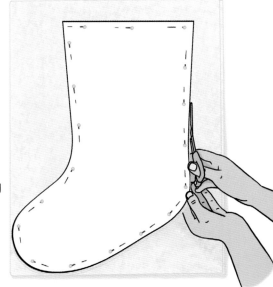

2 Enlarge and copy the heart template on page 125 onto a piece of paper and cut it out. Pin the template to the red felt and cut out a heart to decorate the front of the stocking.

3 Pin the heart to the front of one stocking shape, about halfway down. Following the instructions on page 14, blanket stitch the heart to the stocking using red sewing thread and stitching all the way around.

Don't forget to hang up your STOCKING!

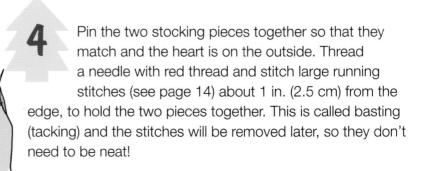

4 Pin the two stocking pieces together so that they match and the heart is on the outside. Thread a needle with red thread and stitch large running stitches (see page 14) about 1 in. (2.5 cm) from the edge, to hold the two pieces together. This is called basting (tacking) and the stitches will be removed later, so they don't need to be neat!

5 Now sew blanket stitch all the way around the edges of the stocking with the red embroidery floss (thread), leaving the straight top edges of the stocking open. Remove the basting threads.

6 Take the piece of gingham fabric. Fold it in half across the width, right sides together, and stitch the short side seam together using small running stitches (see page 14), so that you have a wide band. Turn it right side out and ask an adult to help you press the piece flat using a warm iron.

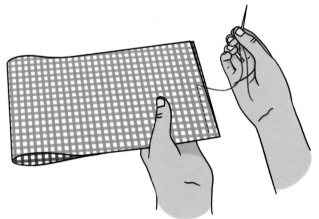

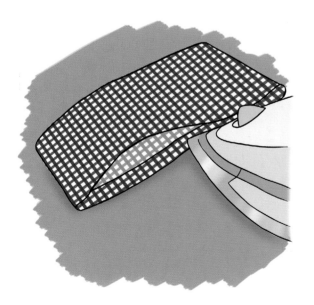

7 Turn under ½ in. (1 cm) of the top and bottom edges to the inside of the gingham and ask an adult to help you press it flat all the way around with an iron—you will have to turn the band as you go.

Tip

The stocking would also work in a bright Christmassy red color. Other jolly variations would be a star or Christmas tree motif on the front of the stocking.

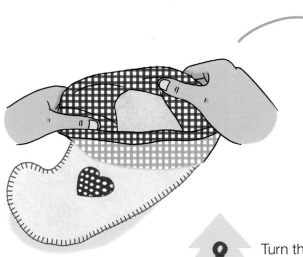

8 Turn the band so the wrong side faces out and push about half of it inside the stocking. Then fold the top half of the band over the top of the stocking to make the cuff. Sew small running stitches all around the top of the stocking to hold it in place.

9 Fold the piece of gingham ribbon in half to form a loop, and stitch it to the inside of the gingham fabric at the back seam of the stocking with a few running stitches. Finish by gluing a small pearl button to the heart.

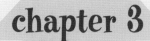

chapter 3
Festive Cards and Wrap

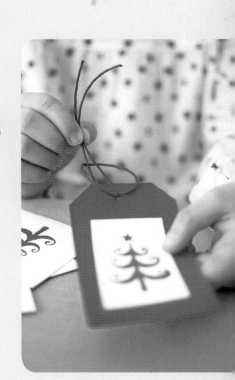

Felt Motif Card

Felt is great for decorating cards, as it comes in a wide selection of colors and does not fray when it is cut. We've made Christmas baubles but you could use any Christmas-themed cookie cutters as templates, or other shapes from the template section on pages 120–125. You can either buy ready-made card blanks to decorate or cut and fold your own from colored card (see page 12).

You will need

A round cookie cutter or small round object

Felt

Pencil

Scissors

Gingham ribbon, ¼ in. (5 mm) wide

White (PVA) glue

Blank cards and envelopes or colored card to make your own (see page 12)

1 Place the cookie cutter on the felt and draw around it with a pencil, or use something small and round to draw around. Carefully cut out the bauble shape. If you are making more than one card, it's a good idea to cut out all your felt shapes at the same time.

2 Cut a piece of gingham ribbon about 2 in. (5 cm) long and fold it into a loop. Glue the ends of the ribbon loop onto the front of the card, just below where the top of the bauble will be positioned. Press down firmly to make sure the loop is glued in place.

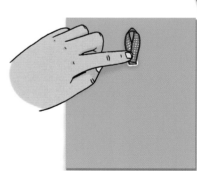

3 Apply a thin layer of glue to the back of the felt bauble shape and stick it onto the card, making sure that you have covered both the ends of the ribbon loop. Press down firmly and let it dry completely.

Have fun with FELT

 **4** To make a ribbon bow, cut a length of ribbon about 4 in. (10 cm) long and follow the instructions on page 13.

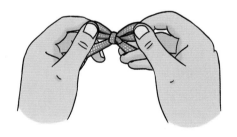

5 Apply a small dab of glue to the back of the bow, and stick it to the front of the bauble. Press down firmly to secure it in place and let it dry completely.

Potato Print Gift Wrap

The presents you give to your friends and family can be even more special if you wrap them in gift wrap you have made yourself. We've used shiny metallic paint and a simple star shape cookie cutter to make a potato print gift wrap, but you can use ordinary paint and other Christmas shapes, such as trees or snowflakes, depending on your cookie cutters.

You will need

Medium-sized potato

Christmas cookie cutter

Cutting board

Sharp knife

Paper towels

Paints

Saucers to hold the paints

Small sponge paint roller

Large sheets of white paper or brown parcel paper

1 Place the potato on a cutting board and with one firm slice, cut the potato in half. The cut surface needs to be as flat as possible. (You may want to ask an adult to help you with the cutting here and in the next step.) Now place the cookie cutter on the board with the sharp edge facing upward. Press the cut surface of one half of the potato firmly down onto the cutter so that the cutter is pushed almost all the way in, with only about ¼ in. (5 mm), still sticking out.

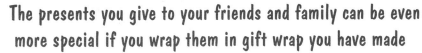

2 Leave the cookie cutter in place and cut away the edges of the potato all around it, using a sharp knife. This needs to be done very carefully, so that the star shape is as clear as possible and you don't cut your fingers! Take off the cookie cutter.

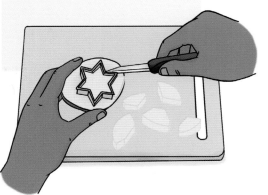

3 Press the potato down onto some paper towels to dry the surface so that the paint doesn't turn watery when you print.

Tip
Use a different cookie cutter shape for the other half of the potato.

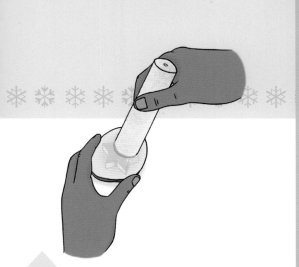

4 Pour the paint into a saucer and use the end of the sponge paint roller to apply the paint to the star shape. Don't put too much paint on the potato, or it will spread out over the edges when you print. Gently blot the potato on a paper towel if you think you've put on too much.

5 Start printing. Press the potato onto the paper and gently rock it from side to side without lifting it from the paper. This will print the shape evenly, even if the cut surface of the potato is not quite flat. Lift straight up and off so you don't smudge it.

6 Keep printing all over the paper, spacing the prints out evenly. Let the paint dry completely before you wrap any presents!

Nordic Reindeer Card ☺☺○

Layer up tissue paper to create this colorful and unusual Christmas card. There's lots of cutting out but don't worry about getting all the tissue shapes too exact—they will look lovely however you cut and stick them, and each card will be different.

You will need

Templates on page 124

Pencil

Scissors

Ruler (a metal one is best but plastic will do)

Sheet of thin white card

Hole punch (optional)

Tissue paper in assorted colors

Glue stick

Sheet of colored card or card blank measuring 5 x 5 in. (13 x 13 cm)

White (PVA) glue

1 Copy the small reindeer template on page 124 onto thin white card. Cut out the reindeer shape, taking care around the fiddly antlers—move the card not the scissors to help cut out the curves. You can use a hole punch to cut out the eye but be careful to get it in the right position.

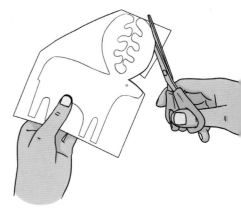

2 Cut out different shapes and colors from tissue paper, using the templates as a guide. You can place the tissue over the template and gently trace the pattern with a light pencil.

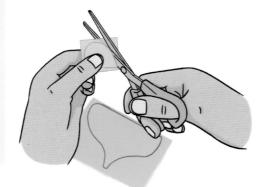

3 Apply glue stick to the tissue paper shapes, taking care as the tissue paper tears easily. Layer the tissue shapes using the photograph and template as a guide.

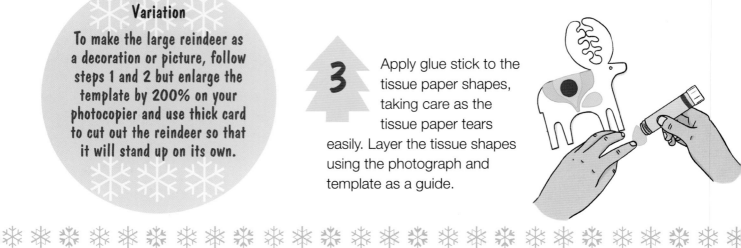

Variation
To make the large reindeer as a decoration or picture, follow steps 1 and 2 but enlarge the template by 200% on your photocopier and use thick card to cut out the reindeer so that it will stand up on its own.

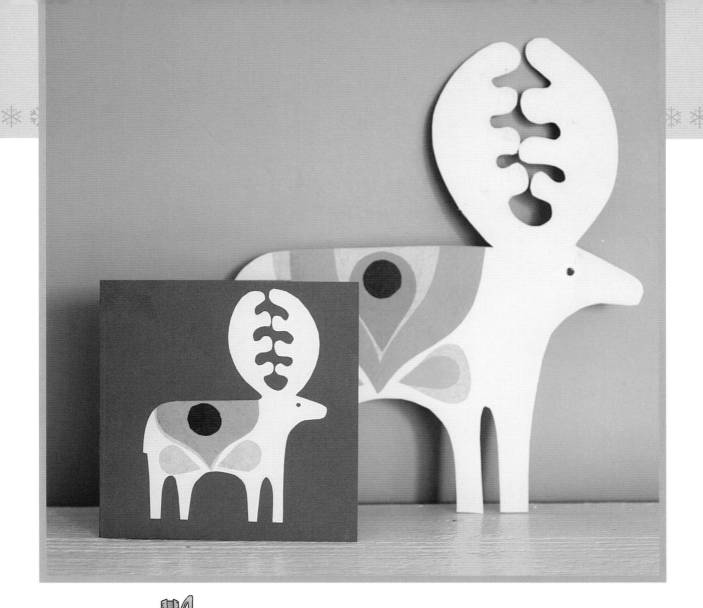

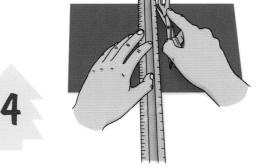

4

To make your own card, cut a piece of colored card to measure 5 x 10 in. (13 x 26 cm). Measure 5 in. (13 cm) along the long sides to find the middle and mark it. Follow the instructions on page 12 to score the crease. Fold the card in half on the scored line. Press the crease down firmly.

5

Stick the reindeer to the front of the card, placing it carefully in the center.

Stenciled Gift Bag

What better way to present a gift than in your very own hand-crafted gift bag? These are made from plain gift wrap and stenciled with a Christmassy candy cane design. You can use a store-bought stencil, or make your own from the templates on pages 120–125. This project needs some accurate measuring and folding, but it's worth it for a professional result.

You will need

Plain gift wrap or paper

Ruler

Scissors

Stencil, either buy one or make your own (see page 11)

White paint

Stencil brush or paintbrush

Paper towels

Double-sided tape

Cardboard

Hole punch

16 in. (40 cm) gingham ribbon (½ in./1 cm wide)

1 Cut a rectangular piece of gift wrap measuring 22 x 13 in. (56 x 33 cm).

2 On the back of the paper, measure 1½ in. (4 cm) in from one long edge and make a mark. Do this in two or three places, join up the dots with a ruler, and then score along this line with your scissors (see page 12) before you fold it in. Make another fold in the same way 3 in. (7 cm) in from the other long edge. Fold in both the shorter ends by ¾ in. (2 cm).

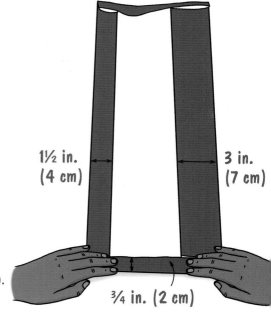

1½ in. (4 cm)

3 in. (7 cm)

¾ in. (2 cm)

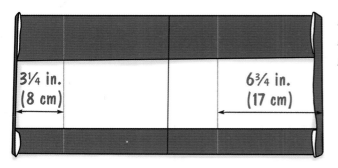

3¼ in. (8 cm)

6¾ in. (17 cm)

3 Now fold the paper in half so the shorter folded edges meet, and press flat, making a sharp crease. Open out again, and on the wrong side of the paper, draw two lines, one 3¼ in. (8 cm) in from one short edge, then another at 6¾ in. (17 cm) from the opposite short edge. Score and then fold the paper along each line. These folds form the box shape of the bag.

BETTER than gift wrap...

4 Lay the bag flat, right side up, with the narrow, turned-in long edge at the top. Attach the stencil to one of the larger panels with masking tape. Dip the brush in the paint and blot on paper towels—you need the brush quite dry. Dab the paint over the stencil. Let the paint dry slightly before removing the stencil. Move it to the other large panel if you want motifs on both sides of the bag.

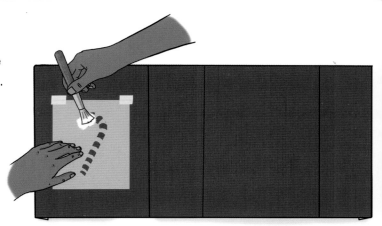

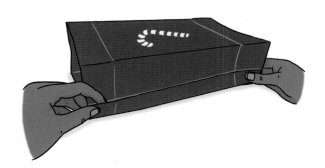

5 Open out the bottom 3 in. (7 cm) fold of the bag but keep the top 1½ in. (4 cm) fold in place. Now fold the bag into its box shape. Stick a line of double-sided tape along one of the folded-in edges where the sides meet, remove the backing paper, and press the other folded-in edge firmly down onto it.

6 Now to fold in the base—this is the trickiest part. Turn the bag onto one of its narrow sides. There is a crease running all the way around the bag 3 in. (7 cm) from the edge. Take the bottom corner closest to you and fold it into the bag so it meets this crease. Line up the corner edge with this crease so that you make a triangle and the base begins to fold in. Press the triangle flat.

7 Turn the bag over onto the other narrow side and do the same at the other end, this time with the corner that is furthest from you.

8 Half the base is now folded in with triangles at both ends. Repeat on the other side to complete the base. Stick the triangles down with double-sided tape.

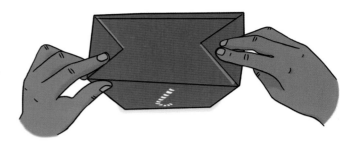

9 Place the bag on a piece of cardboard and draw around the base. Cut out the rectangle, cutting just inside the line, and put it inside the bag to strengthen it.

10 Punch two holes on the front and back of the bag just below the top edge and thread two 8 in. (20 cm) lengths of ribbon through them. Knot the ends on the inside of the bag to hold them in place.

3-D Card

These cards are super easy to make but look really stunning! A simple fold and some careful matching give you an instant 3-D effect.

You will need

Template on page 121

Paper and pencil

Scissors

Scraps of decorative paper or gift wrap

Pinking shears or decorative edge shears

Blank cards or card to make your own (see page 12)

Glue stick

1 Copy the star template on page 121 onto a piece of paper and cut it out. Place the template on the back (plain) side of the decorative paper, and draw around it. Draw two shapes for each card.

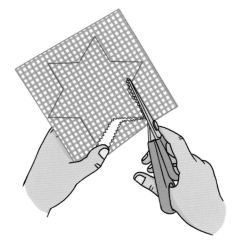

2 Carefully cut out the star shapes. Use pinking shears or other decorative edge craft scissors for a pretty effect.

3 Take one of the paper stars and fold it in half, with the right (patterned) side of the paper facing inward. Make sure the fold is in the center, then press along the crease. This is the 3-D part of the star.

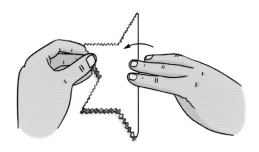

Star LIGHT, star BRIGHT

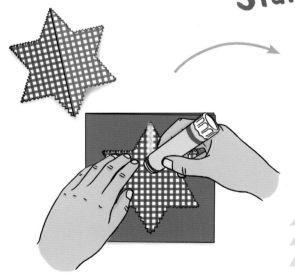

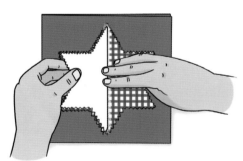

4 Glue the unfolded star to the front of the card with a point at the top. Make sure that all the points are firmly stuck down. Now dab glue all the way down the center of the flat star on the card. Carefully match the fold of the folded star with the line of glue and stick it flat on top of the first star, matching the points of the stars.

5 When the glue is dry, gently bend the flaps of the top star upward, to create a 3-D effect.

Stamped Gift Labels

Homemade labels are so much nicer than store-bought ones. Use pretty Christmas rubber stamps to make these labels and add string ties for a professional look. You could also repeat the pattern on a large sheet of paper to make matching gift wrap.

You will need

....

Card for label

Scissors

Stamping ink pad

Rubber stamp

Glue

Hole punch

White paper or card

6 in. (15 cm) string or twine per label

Squared math paper (optional)

1 Cut out a rectangle of card measuring about 3 x 6 in. (8 x 15 cm). Use scissors to snip off the top two corners of the card on the diagonal, to form the top of the gift label.

2 Cut out small pieces of white paper or card measuring about 2 x 3 in. (5 x 8 cm). Using the foam ink pad, apply some stamping ink to the front of the stamp, making sure the design is completely and evenly covered. Try to avoid getting ink on the face of the stamp block in case it marks the paper.

Tip
If you are going to make a few labels it is easiest to draw two templates on squared paper. Then you can draw around it each time.

3

Get STAMPING!

Place the stamp firmly on the center of a piece of white paper and use a gentle rocking motion to make sure that the design is completely transferred onto the paper. Lift straight off. Let the ink dry completely.

4

Glue the paper design to the front of the label. Use a hole punch to make a hole between the two angled corners of the label.

5

Fold the length of string in half and thread the loop through the hole in the label. Pass the ends of the string through the loop and pull to tighten. Your label is ready for your own hand-written greeting.

Glitter Tree Card

Make some really sparkly Christmas cards using a stencil, some glitter, and some jewel stickers. You can make lots of them for friends and family, but you will need to use shiny, coated card from a packaging box to make a strong, waterproof stencil that you can use over and over again—and you'll need some big pots of glitter too! You can either buy ready-made cards to decorate or cut and fold your own (see page 12).

You will need

Template on page 122

Paper and pencil

Card for stencil—use shiny-coated card from a packaging box

Sharp pointed scissors

Blank cards and envelopes or colored card to make your own (see page 12)

Paper clips or sticky tac

White (PVA) glue

Stencil brush

Glitter in a contrasting color

Jewel stickers

1 Copy the template on page 122 and use it to make a stencil from the shiny card, following the instructions on page 11.

2 Place the tree stencil in the center of the blank card with the shiny side up. Hold it in place with paper clips or small pieces of sticky tac. Using the stencil brush, dab glue into the tree shape. Keep the brush quite dry and hold it upright so that the glue doesn't spread under the card. Make sure you go right to the edges and into the points. Leave the stencil in place.

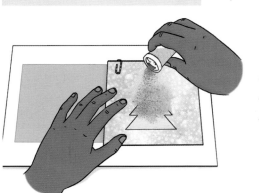

3 Put the card on a big sheet of paper to catch the excess glitter. Sprinkle lots of glitter onto the stencil and leave for about 10 minutes so that the glue begins to dry. Shake off any excess glitter onto the paper and return it to the pot.

Sparkle and SHINE

4 Carefully lift away the stencil to reveal the glittery tree. Finish by decorating the tree with tiny jewel stickers and let it dry completely before sending.

Button Snowman Card

This Christmas card is really simple to make and uses different-size buttons to create a cute snowman. Add arms and a hat brim made from pipe cleaners and an orange felt carrot nose, or make Santa with red and white buttons. Sprinkle on lots of sparkly glitter for a snowy effect.

You will need

....

Blank card or colored card to make your own (see page 12)

3 flat white buttons (small, medium, and large)

White (PVA) glue

Black pipe cleaner

Scraps of orange and black felt for the hat and nose

Paintbrush

White glitter

1 Place the blank card flat on the table and arrange the three buttons on the front to make a snowman. Glue each button in place, keeping them in line.

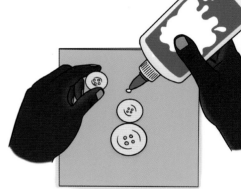

2 From the black pipe cleaner, cut two arms, approximately 1 in. (2.5 cm) long, and a brim for the snowman's hat, measuring about ¾ in. (2 cm). Glue these to the card.

3 Cut a small rectangle from the black felt and glue it to the card to finish the hat. Cut a tiny triangle for the snowman's nose from the orange felt and glue it to the top button. Let it dry thoroughly.

Sort out some SNOWMAN buttons

4 Put your card on a sheet of scrap paper or newspaper. Use the paintbrush to dot small blobs of glue all over the card. Sprinkle the glitter over the blobs to make snowflakes. Gently shake the extra glitter off onto the paper and return it to the pot. Let the glue dry completely before sending your card.

chapter 4
Treat Time!

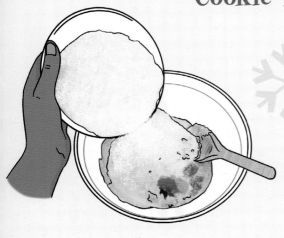

Stained-glass Cookies

Beautiful and tasty too—you can hang these stained-glass snowflake cookies on your tree or in a window to catch the light. The stained glass is made from crushed candies that you melt in the oven!

You will need

1 package boiled candies (sweets) in assorted colors

For 12 vanilla cookies

1⅔ sticks (185 g) unsalted butter, softened

1¼ cups (240 g) superfine (caster) sugar

1 egg

1½ teaspoons vanilla extract

4 cups (390 g) all-purpose (plain) flour

½ teaspoon salt

Equipment

Sifter (sieve)

2 baking sheets

Baking parchment

Rolling pin

Snowflake cookie cutter set

Small Ziplock bags

Cutting board

Toothpicks (cocktail sticks)

Drinking straw

Small palette knife

Ribbon, for hanging

1 Wash your hands with warm water and soap before you begin cooking. To make the cookies, put the butter in a bowl and beat for a couple of minutes with a wooden spoon, then add the sugar and beat well until the mixture is pale and fluffy. Break the egg in a small bowl. Pick out any pieces of shell, then add the egg to the mixture with the vanilla extract, and beat again until creamy.

2 Using a sifter (sieve), sift the flour and salt into a bowl, then add one half of it to the butter mixture and beat until it is completely mixed in. Add the rest of the flour and mix for a few minutes until a dough begins to form and easily comes loose from the sides of the bowl.

3 Sprinkle a little flour onto a clean work surface. Turn the dough out and knead it into a ball. Wrap it in plastic wrap (clingfilm) and put it into the fridge for at least 30 minutes. Ask an adult to turn the oven on to 325°F (160°C) Gas 3. Cut baking parchment to fit each baking sheet.

4 Sprinkle a little flour onto a clean work surface. Take the dough out of the fridge and leave it on the work surface for a few minutes to soften a little, then squash it flat and use the rolling pin to roll it out so that it is about ¼ in.

(5 mm) thick all over—try to get it nice and even and the same shape as one of your baking sheets. Carefully move the sheet of dough to the baking sheet. It's easier to cut out the cookies on the sheet, as the snowflakes will be too delicate to move later.

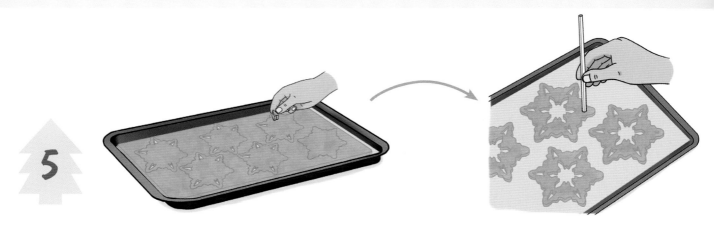

5

Using the cookie cutters, cut out the snowflake shapes and then, using the small insert cutters, cut out snowflake patterns. If some bits of dough don't come out properly, use a toothpick to neaten up the cut-out shapes. Carefully remove the unwanted dough from the edges. Use the end of a drinking straw to cut out a hole at the top of each snowflake—this will be used to thread the ribbon through. Squash all the trimmings together and roll out the dough again. Move this to the second baking sheet and cut out more snowflakes in the same way as before.

6

Put the cookies in the fridge for 10 minutes to chill, then part-bake (only partly cook) the cookies for 6 minutes. Remove the baking sheets from the oven with oven mitts and let the cookies cool on the baking sheets.

7

Separate the boiled candies into piles of different colors. Put each color into a separate Ziplock bag, squeeze out the air, and zip it up. Put it onto a cutting board and smash the candies into small pieces with a rolling pin.

8 Carefully fill each of the snowflake gaps with pieces of smashed candy—don't mix the colors or pile them too high. Pop the cookies back into the oven for a further 5–6 minutes.

9 Remove the baking sheet from the oven using oven mitts. The "glass" parts will be bubbly, but the bubbles disappear as they cool. (Don't touch the "glass" as it will give you a nasty burn.) Leave the snowflakes to cool for at least 20 minutes, then gently slide a small palette knife under each one and lift it onto a cooling rack to go cold.

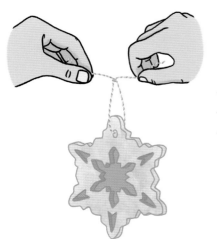

10 When the cookies are completely cool, thread a length of ribbon or cord through the hole, knot the ends together, and your stained-glass snowflake is ready to hang on your tree or in a window.

Catch-the-light COOKIES

Popcorn Garland

Have fun making popcorn and then string it together to make a tasty decoration for your tree or room. You could make it even prettier by adding in some of your favorite candies or sprinkling it with some edible glitter for a bit of sparkle. Make some extra garlands to hang outside as a welcome winter treat for the birds.

You will need

Safflower (sunflower) oil, for frying

A large saucepan with lid (a clear lid so that you can watch the corn popping is more fun)

Popcorn kernels

Oven mitts

Needle (quite a fine sharp one works best)

Brightly colored threads

Small soft candies (optional)

Edible glitter (optional)

1 Put 1 tablespoon of oil in a large saucepan. Ask an adult to help you put it over medium-high heat. Add enough popcorn to cover the base of the pan, put the lid on tightly, and wait for the popping to start. Holding the pan and lid firmly with oven mitts, give the pan a good shake from time to time.

2 When the popping stops, it means that all the kernels have popped and you can turn off the heat and remove the pan from the stovetop (hob). Tip the popcorn into a large bowl and let it cool.

Keep on THREADING

3 Thread the needle with a long piece of colored thread and tie a big, double knot at the end. Carefully push the needle through a piece of popcorn and pull it to the end of the thread. (If the popcorn keeps breaking, try using a finer needle and thread.) Keep threading more pieces until you have a long garland. Remember to add in the candies if you are using them.

4 When your garland is long enough, take off the needle and tie another big knot, or make it into a loop by tying the two ends together. Make lots of garlands with different-colored threads. If you have some edible glitter, put the garlands back in the bowl and sprinkle it all over.

Chocolate Truffles

Make these truffles for a delicious homemade gift. You can choose between covering them simply with a dusting of cocoa or maybe use some sparkly silver balls, or Christmassy sprinkles. Package them up in a little box with some pretty tissue paper.

You will need

3 tablespoons (50 g) unsalted butter, softened

⅓ cup packed (75 g) light brown sugar

⅔ cup (150 ml) heavy (double) cream

6 oz. (175 g) dark chocolate

Toppings

5 oz. (150 g) milk or dark chocolate

And choose from:

Chocolate sprinkles

Colored sprinkles

Cocoa powder

Edible silver balls

Chopped nuts (hazelnuts or slivered/flaked almonds)

A baking sheet, lined with baking parchment

Makes about 20 truffles

1 Put the butter, sugar, and cream in a saucepan and ask an adult to help you place it on the stovetop (hob) over a low heat. Stirring occasionally, leave the pan until the mixture comes to a boil and the sugar has melted. Turn the heat off.

2 Break the chocolate into small pieces and put in a heatproof bowl. Carefully pour the melted butter mixture over the chocolate and stir them together until the chocolate has melted, and the mixture is smooth and shiny.

3 Let the chocolate mixture cool, then cover the bowl with plastic wrap (clingfilm) and put in the fridge to chill for 2–3 hours until it's firm.

4 When firm, scoop a teaspoonful of the chocolate mixture and roll it quickly between your hands into a ball. Place the ball on the lined baking sheet. Before you start and after every four or five truffles, wash your hands in cold water—if your hands are cold it is much easier to roll the truffles!

5 For the toppings, first break up the chocolate into small pieces. Ask an adult to help you put it into a heatproof bowl over a pan of barely simmering water, making sure the bottom of the bowl doesn't touch the water. Stir very carefully until it has melted. Take the bowl off the pan and let it cool slightly.

6 Put each of your chosen toppings onto a separate plate. Take a chocolate ball and dip it in the melted chocolate to coat it all over.

7 Roll the coated ball in one of the toppings, then place it back on the baking sheet to set. Repeat with the remaining truffles and let them set on the baking sheet before serving or packing into a pretty box to give as a gift.

Chocolate HEAVEN!

Tip

Be warned—you will probably end up with chocolate all over you and your kitchen, so wear an apron and remember not to lick your fingers before you have finished!

Marzipan Christmas Figures

Marzipan is a bit like modeling clay except that it tastes much nicer! To make these cute, chunky animals, you need to color your marzipan first and then get modeling. These two are only a start—try a snowman, robin, or Santa. They would all look perfect on top of the Christmas cake or to decorate the table.

You will need

Confectioners' (icing) sugar

7 oz. (200 g) natural white marzipan

Assorted food coloring pastes—for these animals you will need black, brown, red, yellow, and orange

A small cup of water

Makes about 10 figures

Tip

Dip your finger in water and use it as glue to stick the pieces of marzipan together.

To make one penguin

1 Wash your hands well with soap and water. Sprinkle a little confectioners' (icing) sugar on your work surface and then knead the marzipan to soften it—just as you would with modeling clay. Keep the marzipan you aren't working with tightly covered in plastic wrap (clingfilm) to stop it drying out.

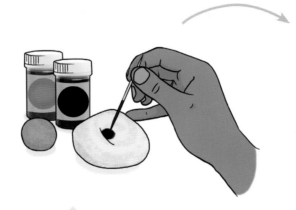

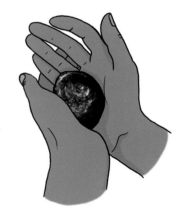

2 To color the marzipan, break off a small piece from the block for the beak and add a drop of orange coloring. Knead it until the color is evenly spread through the marzipan. Next, break off two larger pieces about the size of ping pong balls. Leave one white. Add a few drops of black coloring to the other and knead it until the black is mixed through evenly. Add more coloring if it isn't dark enough.

 **3** Now you are ready to begin modeling. Break off a small amount of white marzipan and keep it to one side for the eyes. Roll the rest of the white marzipan into a ball for the body and put it on a clean work surface. Make a smaller ball with some of the black marzipan for the head. Stick the head on top of the body, using a little water to help them stick together.

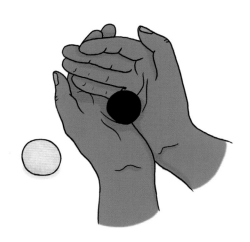

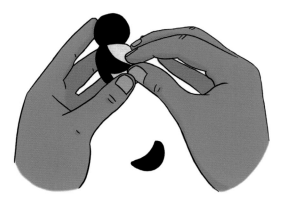

4 Take a piece of the remaining black marzipan and flatten it into a thin disc about the same width as the penguin's body, then wrap it around the back of the penguin. Trim it to shape if you need to before sticking it in place. Take two smaller pieces of black marzipan and shape into wings. Attach them to the side of the body.

 5 Mold some feet out of black marzipan and stick them under the penguin's body so that you can see them clearly.

6 To make the eyes, take some of the white marzipan you put aside in step 3, roll it into two tiny balls, and flatten into discs. Roll two even smaller balls of black marzipan, flatten them, and stick in the middle of the white discs. Attach the eyes to the penguin's face.

7 Roll and pinch the orange marzipan into a beak shape. Stick this onto the penguin's face.

To make one reindeer

1 Follow step 1 on page 102. Then break off four small pieces of marzipan from the block for the reindeer's nose, eyes, and antlers. Add a little red food coloring paste to one piece and knead it until the color is evenly mixed in. Color the other pieces yellow and black in the same way (you may have some black left from the penguin, if you made it—you only need a tiny piece). Leave the fourth piece white. Cover with plastic wrap (clingfilm).

2 Break off a larger piece of marzipan for the reindeer's body and head (a bit bigger than a ping pong ball) and tint it brown. Roll it into two balls— one ball for the body and a smaller ball for the head. Make them more oval than round. Stick the head to the front of the body with a little water.

3 Roll six small nuggets of brown marzipan into balls. Flatten two of them and stick to the top of the head for ears. Make the other four into sausage shapes and stick them around the body for legs—this reindeer is sitting down!

4 Roll a tiny piece of red marzipan into a nose and stick it in place. To make the eyes, follow the instructions in step 6 of the Penguin.

Tip
Color more marzipan if you want to make a whole family of penguins or reindeer!

5 To make the antlers, break off two small nuggets of yellow marzipan and shape into antlers (try a "Y" shape with an extra branch in the middle). Attach to the back of the head behind the ears.

CUTE and tasty!

Peppermint Creams

Peppermint creams are delicious and easy to make, and they need no cooking. Always let them dry on baking parchment before putting them into boxes.

You will need

1¾ cups (225 g) confectioners' (icing) sugar

4–6 tablespoons sweetened condensed milk

½ teaspoon peppermint extract

Green food coloring (optional)

Equipment

Sifter (sieve)

Wooden spoon

Baking parchment

Baking sheet

Rolling pin

Mini star-shaped cutter or any other small cutter

Makes 20–30 peppermint creams

1 Put on an apron and wash your hands well with soap and warm water. Sift the confectioners' (icing) sugar into a large bowl. Gradually add the condensed milk and peppermint extract, mixing with a wooden spoon. The mixture should come together like dough. It is easier to use your hands toward the end of the mixing.

2 Sprinkle some confectioners' sugar onto a clean work surface. Shape the dough into a ball and knead it. To do this put it on the work surface, push it down with your hands and flatten it, fold it over, and turn it around half a turn. Do this again and again for a couple of minutes until your dough is smooth. Sprinkle the surface with more sugar if it sticks.

Tip

Let them dry out overnight before packing into pretty boxes.

3 If you like, you can now divide the dough in half and tint one half green using a few drops of the food coloring. Knead the colored dough again until it is green all over without any streaks.

4 Place a piece of baking parchment onto a baking sheet.

5 On the work surface, roll out the dough to a thickness of ¼ in. (5 mm) using a rolling pin. Stamp out shapes with your cookie cutter and arrange them on the baking parchment. Gather the leftover bits together, knead them again, roll out again, and cut more shapes. Keep doing this until you have used up all your dough.

Pretty PEPPERMINT gift

Gingerbread House

This gingerbread house is straight out of a fairy tale. It's a great activity to help pass the time in the countdown to Christmas and lots of fun to make with friends and family. Practice your piping skills as you stick it together and then choose your favorite candies to decorate it, from chocolate buttons and jellies, to chocolate-coated beans and sprinkles.

You will need

3 cups (375 g) all-purpose (plain) flour

½ teaspoon baking powder

1 teaspoon baking soda (bicarbonate of soda)

3 teaspoons ground ginger

½ teaspoon ground cinnamon

¼ teaspoon each of ground cloves and allspice

A pinch of salt

1 stick (125 g) unsalted butter, softened

⅓ cup (75 g) dark brown soft sugar

1 egg

⅓ cup (100 ml) corn (golden) syrup

2–3 cups (350–500 g) confectioners' (icing) sugar

Assorted candies (sweets)

Equipment

3 baking sheets

A piping bag, fitted with a plain tip (nozzle)

Flat serving tray or platter

A few cans or jars (with food still in them so they are heavy)

Three sheets of squared math paper or plain paper

Pencil and ruler

1 Use a sifter (sieve) and sift the flour, baking powder, baking soda (bicarbonate of soda), ginger, cinnamon, cloves, allspice, and salt together into a mixing bowl and set aside. Put the butter and brown sugar in another bowl and beat them together until they are fluffy. (If an adult is helping you, this is quicker and easier to do with an electric beater.)

2 Break the egg into a small bowl. Pick out any pieces of shell, then mix up the egg with a fork. Add the beaten egg and corn (golden) syrup to the butter and sugar mixture, and mix until smooth. Add the sifted dry ingredients and mix again until smooth.

3 Sprinkle a little flour on a clean work surface. Gather the mixture together into a ball and then put it on the work surface and knead it for a minute or two. Flatten it into a disc, wrap it in plastic wrap (clingfilm), and chill for a couple of hours in the fridge until firm.

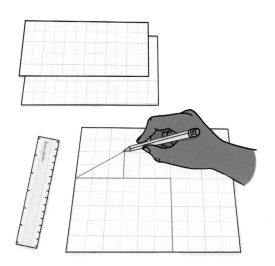

4 While the dough is chilling, make paper templates for the walls and roof of your house. This is easiest if you have some squared paper from a math book, otherwise you will need to use a set square to make sure that your corners are right angles. Draw one rectangle measuring 8 x 4½ in. (20 x 11 cm) for the roof, and another measuring 7½ x 4 in. (19 x 10 cm) for the front and back walls. Now draw a square with sides 4 in. (10 cm) long. Measure to find the middle point of the top edge. Draw a line at right angles to the side measuring 1½ in. (4 cm) up from this point. Join the corners of the square to the top of the line to make a pointy house shape.

5 When you are ready to bake the house, ask an adult to turn the oven on to 350°F (180°C) Gas 4. Use a little butter to rub all over the baking sheets to grease them. This will stop the gingerbread from sticking to them. Now sprinkle more flour on the work surface. Using a rolling pin, roll out the dough to a thickness of about ⅛ in. (3–4 mm).

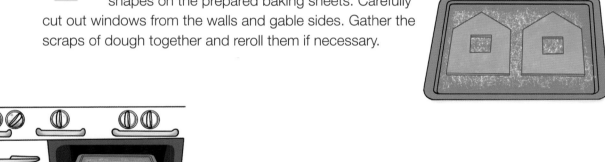

6 Put the paper templates on the dough and use a blunt knife to cut around the shapes. Cut 2 roof shapes, 2 big walls, and 2 gable sides. Arrange the shapes on the prepared baking sheets. Carefully cut out windows from the walls and gable sides. Gather the scraps of dough together and reroll them if necessary.

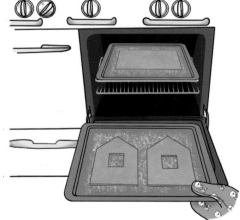

7 Ask an adult to help you put the sheets into the preheated oven. You will need to bake the gingerbread in batches. Bake for about 10–15 minutes until firm and just starting to brown at the edges. Ask an adult to help you remove the gingerbread from the oven and let it cool completely.

8 Use the confectioners' (icing) sugar to make icing according to the manufacturer's instructions. It will need to be thick enough to hold its shape when piped, so add the water gradually until it's like toothpaste! Fill the piping bag with the icing.

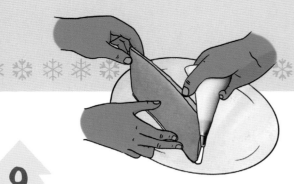

9 You will need two pairs of hands for the next steps as you will be using the icing like glue to glue the pieces together and stick them to the serving tray! Ask your helper to hold one gingerbread house side and pipe a line of icing along the bottom edge and up one side edge. Stand the side wall upright in position on a serving tray or platter. Use a heavy tin or jar to keep it upright.

10 Now ask your helper to hold a gable end piece while you pipe some icing along the bottom edge and two side edges. Position this at a right angle to the first, iced side.

11 Take the second long wall and pipe some icing along the bottom and two sides. Hold this in place opposite the other wall, so that it meets the side at a right angle. Repeat with the remaining gable side. Use more cans or jars inside the house to hold the walls in place until the icing has set.

12 Once the walls are completely set and secure, you can attach the roof. Remove any cans or jars. Pipe a line of icing down the gables and position one roof panel on either side of the gables. Pipe a line of icing across the top of the roof. Hold the roof in place until the icing feels firm.

13 To decorate the house, pipe royal-icing patterns onto the roof panels and decorate with your choice of candies. Pipe on a door and pipe borders around the windows, as well as along the bottom of the house, and decorate with more candies!

Chocolate Money

Do you look for chocolate coins in your stocking each year? Chocolate money is a traditional Christmas candy that kids have been enjoying for generations. Here, you can use a special mold to make extra-special two-tone coins—and licking out the bowl afterward is lots of fun, too!

You will need

3½ oz. (100 g) white chocolate, chopped

8 oz. (225 g) milk or dark chocolate, chopped

Edible glue

Edible gold luster

2 clean paintbrushes

Plastic nozzle bottle

Chocolate coin mold

Waxed (greaseproof) baking parchment

Makes about 20 coins

Tip

If you prefer, use one type of chocolate to fill the mold. In this case, only melt your preferred chocolate and fill the coin mold using either a nozzle bottle or a small pitcher (jug). You will not need to refrigerate the chocolate after filling in the face. Once the mold has been filled, gently tap it to release any air and chill for at least 40 minutes.

1 Ask an adult to help you put the white chocolate in a heatproof bowl over a pan of barely simmering water, making sure the bottom of the bowl doesn't touch the water. Stir very carefully until melted. Let cool slightly.

2 Carefully pour the melted chocolate into a nozzle bottle. Very gently squeeze the bottle to fill a face in the coin mold with the melted chocolate. You want to end up with a clear white chocolate face on a brown chocolate background so try not let any spill over the edge. When all the faces are filled, tap the mold gently to get rid of any air bubbles, and put it in the fridge to chill for 15 minutes.

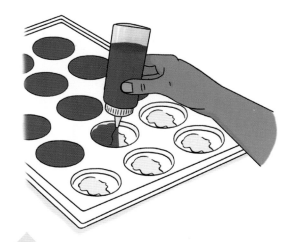

3 Meanwhile, follow the instructions in step 1 to melt the dark or milk chocolate. Once the white chocolate has cooled and set, fill the remainder of the coin mold using either a nozzle bottle or a small pitcher (jug). Gently tap the mold and chill in the fridge for at least 30 minutes.

Christmas COINS galore!

4 When the chocolate has cooled and solidified, gently push out the chocolate coins onto a sheet of waxed (greaseproof) baking parchment. Use a paintbrush to apply a small amount of edible glue onto the coin. With a clean dry brush, gently tap on the edible gold luster. Leave to set.

Marshmallow Snowmen

These cute snowmen are easy and great fun to make, especially with a group of friends to get you in a Christmas party mood. Once you've all made a few, put them together on a serving plate and transform them into a winter wonderland with a dusting of sugar snow.

You will need

7 oz. (200 g) large white marshmallows

Toothpicks (cocktail sticks)

Scissors

Brown or black writing icing

Colored licorice strips or fruit leather

Chocolate-coated mint sticks or pretzel sticks

Large chocolate drops or buttons

4 oz. (100 g) white mini-marshmallows

Confectioners' (icing) sugar, for dusting

Makes about 10 snowmen

1 Place the large marshmallows on a tray or baking sheet. Carefully push 2 large marshmallows onto each toothpick (cocktail stick). Ask an adult to trim off any of the toothpick that is poking out of the top.

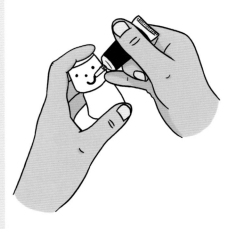

2 Using the writing icing, pipe dots and lines of icing onto the face to make the eyes, nose, and mouth.

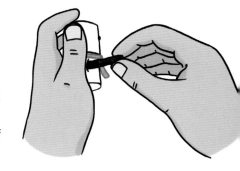

3 Cut the licorice strips or fruit leather into thin strips and carefully tie a strip around the snowman's neck for a scarf. To make the arms, break the chocolate-coated mint sticks in half and push into the sides of the large marshmallow body.

Make your OWN Frosty the Snowman!

4 Pipe a small blob of icing onto the top of the snowman's head and position a large chocolate drop on top. Pipe another blob of icing in the middle of the chocolate drop and stick a mini-marshmallow on the very top. Use the writing icing again to pipe dots down the front of the snowman to look like buttons.

5 Keep making snowmen until you have as many as you need to make a fabulous winter wonderland! To serve, use a sifter (sieve) to scatter confectioners' (icing) sugar over the serving dish to look like snow, arrange the snowmen on top, and dust lightly with a little more sugar.

Cookie Tree Decorations

Decorate these delicious Christmas cookies with colorful writing icing. Make them with your friends, serve them at a party, or string them with pretty ribbons and tie them to your tree—you can always eat them later!

You will need

6 tablespoons (75 g) unsalted butter

½ cup (115 g) superfine (caster) sugar

1 extra large (large) egg

1½ cups (200 g) all-purpose (plain) flour

½ teaspoon baking powder

½ teaspoon salt

Equipment

Plastic wrap (clingfilm)

Baking sheet

Baking parchment

Rolling pin

Cookie cutters in different shapes

Plastic drinking straw

Cooling rack

Tubes of colored writing icing

8 in. (20 cm) ribbon or ricrac braid per cookie

Makes about 18 cookies

1 Put the butter and sugar in a mixing bowl and mix together well with a wooden spoon until the mixture is soft, creamy, and pale. Firmly tap the egg on the side of a separate bowl and pull the two halves apart with your fingertips. Pick out any pieces of shell and then stir into the mixture.

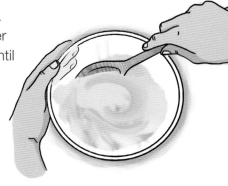

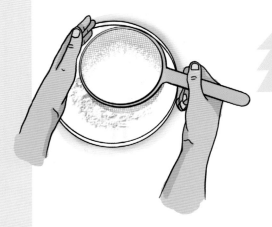

2 Put a sifter (sieve) over the mixing bowl and sift in the flour, baking powder, and salt.

3 Stir everything together until the flour is mixed in and the mixture forms a ball of dough. Stop mixing as soon as the flour is mixed in. Wrap the ball of dough in plastic wrap (clingfilm), and put in the refrigerator for about an hour.

4 When the dough is well chilled, ask an adult to turn the oven on to 350°F (180°C) Gas 4. Put a little soft butter on a piece of paper towel and rub it all over the baking sheet to grease it, then line it with baking parchment.

5 Sprinkle a clean work surface with a little flour and roll out the cookie dough until it is about ½ in. (1 cm) thick. Use the cookie cutters to cut out different shapes, cutting them as close together as possible. When you have cut out the first batch, gather all the trimmings together, roll them out again, and cut out some more. Put the shapes on the lined baking sheet.

6 Push the end of the drinking straw into the top of each shape to make a hole. Bake the cookies for about 8–10 minutes or until golden brown. Watch them carefully—it is easy to burn them. Remove the cookies from the oven. Use the plastic drinking straw to re-pierce the holes if they have closed up during cooking—you need to do this before they cool and while they are still soft. Place the cookies on a wire cooling rack and let cool.

Decorate with DOTS!

 **7** Use dots of writing icing to decorate the cookies. Thread pieces of ribbon or ricrac braid through the holes in each cookie, tie in a knot, and trim the ribbon ends diagonally with scissors to stop them fraying.

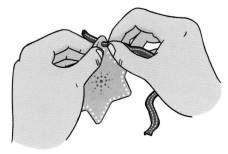

Templates

All the templates for the projects are included here, either at full size (100%) so that you can simply trace them (see page 10) or photocopy them, or at half the proper size (50%)—this means you need to ask an adult to help you to photocopy the template at double the size, using the 200% zoom button on the photocopier.

Pompom Angel-head page 30 (100%)

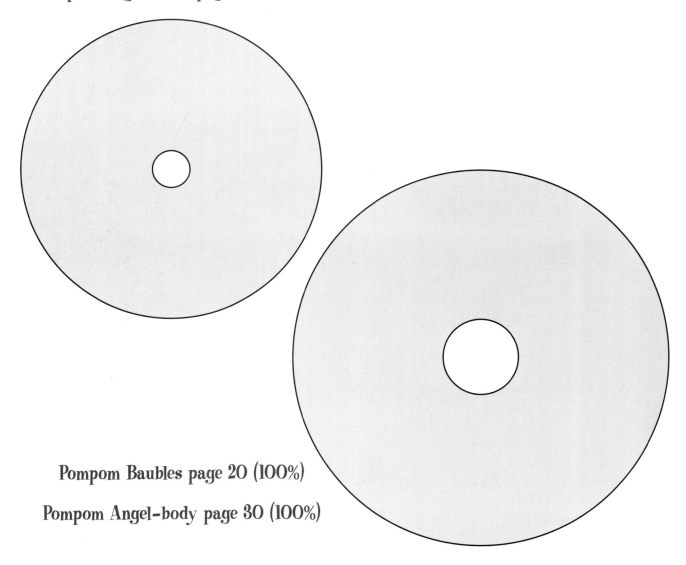

Pompom Baubles page 20 (100%)

Pompom Angel-body page 30 (100%)

Hanging Felt Stars page 26 (100%)

3-D Card page 82 (100%)

Advent Gift Buckets page 42 (100%)

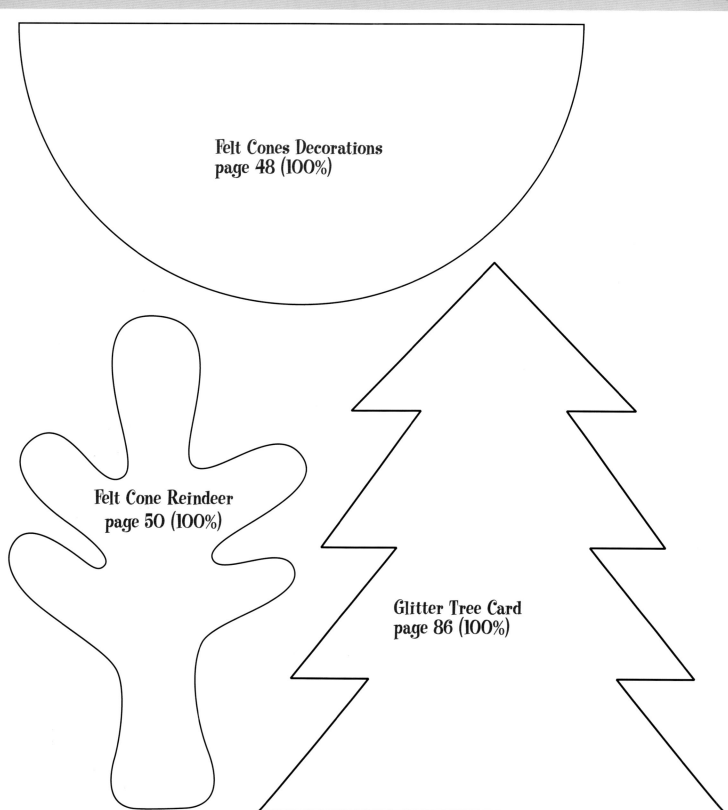

Felt Cones Decorations
page 48 (100%)

Felt Cone Reindeer
page 50 (100%)

Glitter Tree Card
page 86 (100%)

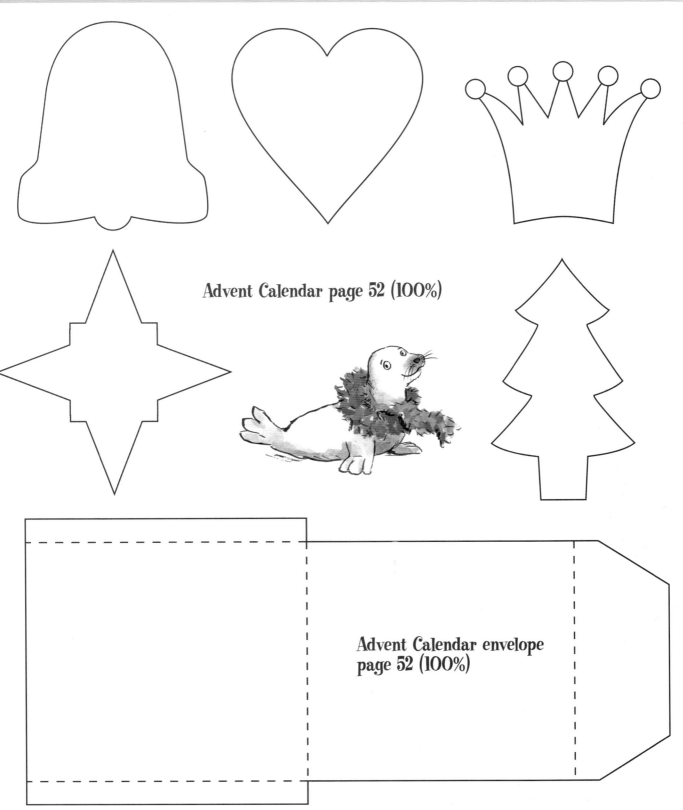

Advent Calendar page 52 (100%)

Advent Calendar envelope
page 52 (100%)

Paper Snowflakes page 56 (100%)

Nordic Reindeer Card page 76 (50%)

Christmas Stocking page 66 (50%)

Suppliers

US

A C Moore
www.acmoore.com

Create for Less
www.createforless.com

Creative Kids Crafts
www.creativekidscrafts.com

The Cookie Cutter Company
www.cookiecuttercompany.com

Darice
www.darice.com

Fancy Flours
www.fancyflours.com

Hobby Lobby
www.hobbylobby.com

Jo-ann Fabric & Crafts
www.joann.com

Michaels
www.michaels.com

Mister Art
www.misterart.com

Walmart
www.walmart.com

UK

Baker Ross
www.bakerross.co.uk

Cakes Cookies and Crafts
www.
cakescookiesandcraftsshop.
co.uk

Early Learning Centre
www.elc.co.uk

Homecrafts Direct
www.homecrafts.co.uk

Hobbycraft
www.hobbycraft.co.uk

John Lewis
www.johnlewis.co.uk

Lakeland
www.lakeland.co.uk

Mulberry Bush
www.mulberrybush.co.uk

The Works
www.theworks.co.uk

Yellow Moon
www.yellowmoon.org.uk

Index

Photographers

Caroline Arber pp. 2, 4-5, 9B, 11, 31-32, 38, 43-55, 59, 70, 87-90
Cath Armstrong pp. 19B, 25, 37, 39TR, 65, 117-119
James Gardiner p. 77
Lisa Linder pp. 3BL, 9T, 91TL, 91BR, 97-109, 115
Debbie Patterson p. 23
Claire Richardson pp. 6, 57
Stuart West pp. 3TR, 91TR, 93-95, 113
Polly Wreford pp. 1, 7-8, 13, 18, 19R, 21, 27-29, 33-35, 39BL, 41, 61-62, 67-69, 71, 73-75, 79-85

Project Makers

Libby Abadee and Cath Armstrong pp. 19 B, 25, 37, 39TR, 65, 117-119
Tessa Evelegh pp. 53-55
Emma Hardy p. 23
Annie Rigg pp. 3BL, 9T, 91TL, 91BR, 96-109, 115
Laura Tabor pp. 3TR, 91TR, 92-95, 113
Catherine Woram pp. 1-2, 4-5, 6-8, 9B, 10-13, 18, 19R, 21, 26-29, 31-35, 38, 39BL, 40-51, 59-62, 66-70, 71, 72-75, 78-90
Clare Youngs pp. 6, 57, 77